^ Poems of Majnun ^

^ Poems of Majnun ^

(Qays Ibn al-Mulawwah 664-688)

Translation & Introduction

Paul Smith

New Humanity Books

BOOK HEAVEN
Booksellers and Publishers

newhumanitybooks@hotmail.com

NEW HUMANITY BOOKS
BOOK HEAVEN
(Booksellers & Publishers for over 40 years)
47 Main Road Campbells Creek 3451 Victoria
Australia

ISBN: 978-1480103870

Poetry/Mysticism/Sufism/Arabian Literature/
Middle Eastern Studies

>CONTENTS<

THE LIFE, TIMES & POEMS OF MAJNUN (QAYS)

Majnun (meaning 'madman') or... Qays ibn al-Mulawwah ibn Muzahim (664-688) was a Bedouin poet in the seventh century of the Bani Amir tribe in the Najd desert. He fell in love with Layla bint Mahdi ibn Sa'd from the same tribe when they were children, she was better known as Layla al-Amiriya.

He soon began composing poems about his love for her, mentioning her name often. Finally, when he asked for her hand in marriage her father refused as this would mean a scandal for Layla, according to local traditions. Some time later, Layla was forced to marry another man.

When Qays heard of her marriage, he fled the tribe camp and began wandering the surrounding desert. His family eventually gave up on his return and left food for him in the wilderness. He could sometimes be seen reciting poetry to himself or writing in the sand with a stick.

Layla moved to present-day Iraq with her husband, where she became ill and eventually died.

Qays was later found dead in the wilderness in 688 near an unknown woman's grave (some say *on* her grave). He had carved three couplets of poetry on a rock near the grave, which are the last three verses attributed to him.

Many other minor incidents happened between his madness and his death. Most of his recorded poetry was composed before his descent into madness. From Arab and Habib folklore the story passed into Persian literature.

The story of Layla and Majnun was known in Persian at least from the time of Rudaki who mentions the lovers. Although the story was somewhat popular in Persian literature in the 12th century, it was the Persian masterpiece of Nizami that popularised it dramatically in Persian literature.

Nizami collected both secular and mystical sources about Majnun and portrayed a vivid picture of the famous lovers.

In the Arabic work of Abulfaraj al-Isfahani (died. 967), the *Kitab al-Aghani,* there is a chapter of over ninety pages on the young poet Qays or Majnun, the lover of Layla.

Other books earlier contained stories about the young lovers but the greatest source for the great Persian poet Nizami's telling of their tale must have come from the collected poems of Qays ibn al-Mulawwah (Majnun) himself.

Subsequently, hundreds of other Persian, Turkish and Urdu poets imitated him or wrote their own versions of the story.

Selected Bibliography

Diwan Majnun Leyla edited by Abd al-Sattar Ahmad Farraj. Makfabat Misr, Cairo, 1973.

Majnun Leyla: Poems about Passion, Translation & Introduction by Joyce Akesson, Pallas Athena, Lund, 2009.

Majnun Laila Translated by George Wightman and Abdullah al-Udhari, T.R. Press, London 1973.

Layla & Majnun by Nizami: Translation, Introduction & Notes by Paul Smith, New Humanity Books, Campbells Creek, 2006.

Classical Arabic Poetry: 162 poems from Imrulkais to Ma'arri, Translated with an Introduction by Charles Greville Tuetly, KPI Limited, London, 1985 (Pages 36-7, 151-3).

A Narration of Love: An Analysis of the Twelfth Century Persian Poet Nizami's Layli and Majnun by A.A. Seyed-Gohrab. Netherlands 2001.

Majnun: The Madman in Medieval Society by M.W. Dols, edited by D.E. Immish. Clarendon Press, 1992.

Love, Madness and Poetry: An Interpretation of Majnun Legend by A. Khairallah. Beirut. 1980.

Leyla and Mejnun by Fuzuli... Translated by Sofi Huri. Introduction and Notes by Alessio Bombaci. George Allen & Unwin Limited 1970. (Of special interest is chapter 3 'The Legend of Majnun' containing some of Qays' poems)

The Poetry of Nizami Ganjavi: Knowledge, Love, and Rhetoric. Edited by Kamran Talattoff and Jerome W. Clinton. Palgrave, 2000. (Chapter 1... 'A Comparison of Nizami's Layli and Majnun and Shakespeare's Romeo and Juliet).

Laila & Majnun: Letters Delivered & Undelivered by Muhammad Salem, International Publications, Lahore, 1937.

The Qit'a: Anthology of the 'Fragment' in Arabic, Persian & Eastern Poetry, Translation & Introduction by Paul Smith, New Humanity Books, Campbells Creek, 2012. (Pages 50-60).

Arabic Poetry

In addition to the eloquence and artistic value, pre-Islamic poetry constitutes as a major source for classical Arabic language both in grammar and vocabulary and as a reliable historical record of the political and cultural life of the time. Poetry held an important position in pre-Islamic society with the poet filling the role of historian, soothsayer and propagandist. Words in praise of the tribe /qit'a/ and lampoons denigrating other tribes seem to have been some of the most popular forms of early poetry. The poet represented an individual tribe's prestige and importance in the Arabian peninsula and mock battles in poetry would stand in lieu of real wars. 'Ukaz, a market town not far from Mecca, would play host to a regular poetry festival where the craft of the poets would be exhibited.

Among the most famous poets of the pre-Islamic era are Imru' al-Qais, al-Nabighah al-Dhubyani, Tarafah ibn al 'Abd , and Zuhayr ibn Abî Sûlmâ. Other poets, such as Ta'abbata Sharran, al-Shanfara, 'Urwah ibn al-Ward, were known as vagabond poets, much of whose works consisted of attacks on the rigidity of tribal life and praise of solitude. Some of these attacks on the values of the clan and of the tribe were meant to be ironic, teasing the listeners only in order finally to endorse all that the members of the audience held most dear about their communal values and way of life. While such poets were identified closely with their own tribes, others, such as al-A'sha, were known for their wanderings in search of work from whoever needed poetry.

The very best of these early poems were collected in the 8th century as the *Mu'allaqat* meaning 'the hung poems' (because they were hung on or in *Kaaba*) and the *Mufaddaliyat* meaning al-Mufaddal's examination or anthology. The *Mu'allaqat* also aimed to be the definitive source of the era's output with only a single example of the work of each of the so-called 'seven renowned ones', although different versions differ in which 'renowned ones' they chose. The *Mufaddaliyat* on the other hand contains rather a random collection.

There are several characteristics that distinguish pre-Islamic poetry from the poetry of later times. One of these characteristics is that in pre-Islamic poetry more attention was given to the eloquence and the wording of the couplet than to the poem as whole. This resulted in poems characterized by strong vocabulary and short ideas but with loosely connected verses. A second characteristic is the romantic or nostalgic prelude with which pre-Islamic poems would often start. In these preludes, a thematic unit called nasib, the poet would remember his beloved and her deserted home and its ruins. This concept in Arabic poetry is referred to as 'standing at the ruins' because the poet would often starts his poem by saying that he stood at the ruins of his beloved.

These early poems were to some extent considered a threat to the newly emerging faith of Islam and if not actually suppressed, fell into disuse for some years. The poets and their pronouncements were too closely associated with the religion practiced before Islam, and the role of the poet was singled out for criticism in the *Koran*. They also praised subjects of dubious merit such as wine, sex and gambling, which clashed with the new ideology. Satirical poems attacking an idea or leader were less censured. While some poets were early converts, poetry about or in praise of Islam took some time to develop.

It was the early poems' importance to Islamic scholarship, though, which would lead to their preservation. Not only did the poems illuminate life in the early years of Islam and its antecedents but they would also prove the basis for the study of linguistics of which the *Koran* was regarded as the pinnacle.

The settled, comfortable and luxurious life in Ummayyad courts led to a greater emphasis on the *ghazal* or love poem. Chief amongst this new breed of poet was Abu Nuwas. Not only did Abu Nuwas spoof the traditional poetic form of the *qasida* and *qit'a* and write many poems in praise of wine, his main occupation was the writing of ever more ribald *ghazal,* some heterosexual and others openly homosexual.

While Abu Nuwas produced risqué but beautiful poems, many of which pushed to the limit what was acceptable under Islam, others produced more religiously themed poetry.

The Sufi tradition also produced poetry closely linked to religion. Sufism is a mystical interpretation of Islam and it emphasised the allegorical nature of language and writing. Many of the works of Sufi poets appear to be simple *ghazal or qit'as.* Under the guise of the love or wine poem they would contemplate the mortal flesh and attempt to achieve transcendence. Rabia al-Adawiyya, Abd Yazid al-Bistami and Mansur al-Hallaj are some of the most significant Sufi poets, but their poetry and doctrine were considered dangerous and al-Hallaj was eventually executed for heresy.

Qays ibn al-Mulawwah or Majnun of 'Majnun and Layla' fame, the subject of this book, composed romantic *qit'as* that soared into pure mysticism and inspired the poetry of Nizami, Jami, Fuzuli and so many others (as will be seen in a following chapter of this Introduction.

A large proportion of all Arabic poetry is written using the monorhyme, *qasida* or *qit'a*. While this may seem a poor rhyme scheme for people used to English literature it makes sense in a language like Arabic that has only three vowels that can be either long or short.

The Form & Function of the *Qit'a*

The *qit'a*, which literally means 'fragment', began in Arabic poetry in pre-Islamic times and then passed on to Persian poetry, then Turkish, Urdu and Punjabi and other Eastern poetry. It must consist of at least two couplets and is similar to a *ghazal* or a *qasida* being a monorhyme, with the second lines of the couplets all having the same rhyme... but in the first couplet the double-rhyme does not appear (hence ab, bb, cb, db, eb etc). It can be composed in any metre except that of the *ruba'i*.

It can be a fragment from a *qasida* (a long poem, sometimes hundreds of couplets) or a *ghazal* (usually between seven and fifteen couplets) that are both with the rhyme pattern of aa, ba, ca, da, ea, fa, ga, ha, etc; or... it may be complete in itself, as it most often was.

Hafiz often used this form to write obituaries on people whom he knew, as did many other poets. It is usually used to insult, complain in a witty manner (sometimes obscenely as with Obeyd Zakani, Abu Numas and others). Some are also philosophical, ethical or meditative. Often the poets would express in this form their own experiences or use it to communicate through letters.

"The qit'a was popular for use in improvisations, a touchstone for new poets, but also a harbour of refuge for their more experienced colleagues who were so frequently required to dispel the peevishness and boredom of their masters." Jan Rypka (see below).

Many in Persian were 'court poems' and many of the early Arabic qit'as were mystical or composed by Sufi Masters such as Mansur al-Hallaj. The poets Qays (Majnun), Abu Nuwas, al-Ma'arri, Anvari, Ibn Yamin are cited as 'masters' of this form.

Sources...

A Literary History of Persia By Edward G. Browne. Volume 2 Cambridge University Press 1902 (Page 34).
Early Persian Poetry by A.V. Williams Jackson: Macmillan New York. 1920.
Borrowed Ware: Medieval Persian Epigrams, Translated by Dick Davis. Mage Publishers, 1997. (Page 23).
History of Iranian Literature: Jan Rypka et al. D. Reidel Publishing Company Holland 1968. (Pages 95-6).

Qita's...

When she was still an innocent girl my love for Layla started:
her growing breasts not noticed by those of her age… or clan.
And when we were children we took the animals out together:
if only we had like those animals, to grow up had never began.

Fearing her parents, with her eyes she told me:
it did not need words, her message of sadness.
Yet, I knew that her eyes were greeting me…
inviting my fascinated soul with love's caress.

By these walls, these walls of Layla I'm passing

and now I'm kissing the wall, this wall of Layla.

It's not love of this house that's taken my heart,

but of that one who dwells in that house, Layla!

I dream that I see us... two gazelles grazing
in remote places, like the plains of *h'awzan.* *
I dream that I see us in the desert: two doves
flying to our nest... as the night came down.
As two fish in the sea I dream and think we
see when the sea lulls us, as evening began.
I dream I see us... my life, your life together!
I see, I dream... even death, unites us again
on the bed of the tomb... lying, side by side.
Retreat from the world, O falls well hidden!
We shall see, when resurrected, a new life...
universe as one, meeting, in the eternal plan.

Note: A herb.

The Amirite Layla, sways back and forth on the camel's back:
those long curls of hers with a silken ribbon she tied together.
When on the top of her hair her comb moves her dark curls...
from them scent of pink amber and sweet basil, does scatter.

O gentle breeze, you are now so cruel to me...
there was a time, happiness you would bring.
O breeze... if in this world only one existed
who love tired out, I am that one, that thing!
If a killer poison with her saliva was stirred,
a drop's all I need to my thirst be quenching.

Pure white, shining like moon in night of whitest frost:

a true beauty to see, but, always beauty's cost is, envy.

Crystal tears keep on reflecting black pupils brilliance:

in darkness, compared to them antimony one can't see.

She's such a good girl that if one becomes too talkative

she becomes shy, and when speaking… speaks, briefly.

Loving heart, don't suffer, die soon full of grief:
in this world our suffering must end eventually.
O my heart, you're in love with a particular one
whom you can only be united with, in Eternity.
Keep on working to discover a way to that one
who in this world has to not be near you, daily.
You love that one with a face like a gazelle's...
whose sun-like beauty brings all eyes... to see!
On fire is your soul and in agony is your heart,
from loving that one your tears rain constantly.
This is the truth... this weeping of yours is the
proof that you love that fine, pure girl... truly!
O, I long for those joyful days to come back…
ah no, the past never comes back, believe me.
Listen, try to be firm, seek out encouragement:
time will not destroy love, it stronger will be!
Layla is far off... will I see her one more time?
Her soul is corrupted by all those full of envy!
O heart, how much more agony can you take?
God, I can't take more, I beg for Your mercy!

This heart of mine feels like it's clutched in the ever tightening talons of some bird... whenever that name of... 'Layla', I hear. It is like ends of the earth are a ring's band impressing me, and no space in length, breadth, width, depth, to exist... can I bear!

My passion for Layla with more of Layla I have treated:

as a drunkard takes more wine to treat in his head, pain.

Can it be possible that Layla believes I do not love her?

I do... 'By the ten days, and even and uneven,'... again!*

*Note: Koran lxxxix, 2-3.

Wrapped in their cowls, through the night the pilgrims
in Mecca call out to God to forgive the sins they recite.
I called, "God, all I want is Layla, that will satisfy me!
If given her, I will repent to You... with all my might!"

Wonderful Najd! Sweet-smelling is Najd's earth,

and if it remains the same, all those who live there!

O mountains of Qana, when will I praise you two:

I left long ago, is it the same there? Change I fear!

You too I remember as night comes, desert flower,

moist from dawn's dew, is it from the night's tear?

Layla, are you still between al Batil and al-Hima,

or young woman, have you moved... to elsewhere?

The breeze smelling of lavender is in my memory

as I wonder if it is passing Najd, through there?

And when I'm on a lean horse that's moving fast

I wish to feel it again all through my flowing hair!

Ah, let me hear again from valley to valley in the

green meadows the groaning of the camels, there.

If I'm going to journey it will only be to the north,

and lightning hitting Yemen, is the kind I prefer.

A man would even kill himself for one like Layla,

even if one like I have learned to live with despair!

If dreaming of peacefulness is significant to do…

Layla, then I need to meet with you, without her.

This body of mine has become wretched, weak…

from dawn until night I'm melancholy's prisoner.

"Where's that prisoner?" love's courier calls out!

"He never gives up: tell, how much can he bear?"

If heart keeps on loving, the hurt will be great…

O death, hold, for my promise is that of a lover!

All you who harass me, know what I go through:
how I pass each day of my life in this wilderness.
The grey partridge has become a friend of mine...
around me, the wild animals eat, them... I bless.
By her life I swear... that, every day all I can do
is in the sand draw her, and listen to the stones.
All these wild animals have become my friends,
no matter if female, male, the oldest, or suckles!
Of the cruel loneliness I'll not tell, or this desert
life I live or how I love her. O painful loneliness!

All who love are the only good people that exist...
all those without love create nothing worthwhile.
If I scold her she says to me, "By your life I swear
that all I want is that we're together, we reconcile.
So, come to my door if you are longing for this one,
for my longing for you is stronger... all the while."

See... when I am reciting the ritual prayers day and night

I face where she is, even if behind me is the place to pray!

But, I don't believe in more than one God: my love for her

is a choking, closing of throat no doctor can cure any day.

I pray... but when I am remembering her I do not know if

I've at morning, twice, eight times faced her way, to pray.

I have not gone to her to be cured through looking at her...

I look at her, leave worse than before... no cure, does stay.

If that one is leaving, then I will surely die:

if that one's coming near, again I am living.

The eastern breeze brings pain to my heart:

then all my eyes do for Layla is… weeping.

That one, Layla, keeps on living in my soul;

this soul, that many a trouble is devouring.

I know that a hand has captured my heart:

blood over its nails, it goes deeper, hurting!

They told to me this: "If you wanted to, you could help…
elsewhere look," and I answered, "No, please don't start!
The love I have for her of my heart has taken possession,
even if it's held back, it is for ever… it will never depart!"

It surprises me that Layla's able to get to sleep

while I can't sleep anymore even if I try hard to.

One time I became sleepy... even though I was

tormented by separation, through and through:

then, my Layla came to me, so beautiful to see

that waking, I almost passed away... it is true!

Layla's spirit visited me after she'd gone away,

I forgot all my complaining, thoughts of me too.

The day she left I wasn't allowed to see her,

but… these weeping eyes told her goodbye.

They said I wasn't allowed to speak to her!

Do not see a heart's goodbye, a lover's cry!

Layla, I greet you… may God protect you

from the sun's rise, until it leaves our sky.

In its clothes, your body is in beauty and joy, radiant!
O Layla, I wish that its reviving light could wake me.
I saw you, yes I saw you, but was it a dream of mine?
Perhaps, it was in daylight… you with love I did see!
And, when I held you I said, "Ah… my fire is dying!"
Then I find it doesn't, it's burning even more fiercely!

Morning bird, fly, to that one carry my greeting:

this greeting to that one now please be carrying.

Let me have some hope when I am calling out...

and let God towards that one... you be taking.

When going back to earth let it be Layla's land,

a desert in which my heart and soul I am losing.

I'm dreaming of a day when we're not separated:

that dream I stay alive for, upon it I am hoping.

Layla, I'm famous from this love I have for you:
of this suffering of mine all the world's hearing.
By such cruel longing I'm trapped, in despair...
I suffer so much, but... who can, me, be saving?
Layla, my desire, whose look fired up my heart,
if you send me off, my life also will be passing!
You are really my Layla? I'll be so kind to you!
Your loving prisoner I am, so me, be believing!
Soul of mine has been so enlivened by my love
that from fear of some envious rival I'm hiding:
some slanderer who might go and tell all of the
people all that they were not already knowing!

Her eyes spoke to me when looking at me;
and so, without speaking my eyes replied.
Her eyes foretold, "Again we will meet:"
but in those eyes it was my death I spied.
I die from fear and hopelessness and I am
born once more out of hope after I've died.
Around me here and there are many men
and genie too, but I don't from them hide.
They can't stop me from seeing you even
if they tried... I'd soon come to your side.

A miserable day it is, this day of goodbye!
She said, "In God's hands I'll leave you!"
Now, that I'm alone in my soul's silence,
my heart can't hold back from loving you.
O God Almighty, my life is leaving me:
she leaves, I cannot stop her... can You?
Friends when I go find where I lie, go to
Layla, say: "You went: he died, for you."

O heart of mine, you may die of sorrow... but, don't fear:
that one who among men does fear, Eternity is not there.
You're in love with a girl that if given... you've Paradise:
try finding a way to where it's impossible to... get there.
I love Najd, of ever returning there I despair, each night.
No Layla, no Najd! Until Resurrection takes me there!

They said to me, "You could forget her if you wanted to!"

I replied, "I don't want to and if I did, I could not, for this

love for Layla to my heart's fastened like bucket in a well

to a rope and soul knows power of such a love as this is."

Still... they go on mocking me, criticizing, sending me off

as they understand that those words... I cannot dismiss.

O sun, Layla and her family you'll be greeting:

please tell me when it will be, dawn or sunset?

When I pass Layla's abode, they hit her: why?

Is it her fault this wolf's mind on there is set?

If anger has to be appeased, stone me when I

say, "Wolf goes, I am no longer any threat."

That water that someone else offers might be sweet and my thirst may be quenched if I wanted, but it I don't try! All the passion of my love is dedicated only to that one, though I am certain my fate by her refusal will be, to die.

I know I will be eventually killed by again lapsing into love...
but, such relapses in the beginning were for me the only gain.
I am given blows that will kill me because of my desperation:
hope smiles in such a way, life I'll continue through this pain.

Ah Layla, I love you, I continue to you…

yet, far off or close by, you won't see me.

Ah Layla, I love you... my slightest sigh

that a breeze could take would bring the

soul of one passing, inhaling... into pain.

I complain of this need alone and openly.

And in silence of my soul I reveal to her

about sadness in my heart... constantly.

And if to her I pray she doesn't hear my

prayers, so then to God I pray, silently.

If near me I see her, all I have are tears...

it's terrifying when in love, passionately.

That one who I should forget in my soul is living...
I can't stop thinking of her when I'm sad or happy.
The evil ones who slander me are only hurting her:
she fear them, sends me off, but in heart keeps me!
The great expanse of my land has narrowed now...
because of Layla I have no friend now to go to see.
For the sake of her those not loving me I've loved:
all who love me I now never see... unfortunately!
It is her camp, who I love, my enemies are there:
will I now run away, or will I her now try to see?
From love's secret agony how will I ever escape?
For it's the only joy heart has, one choice for me!
I fell in love a long time ago, all of that is dead...
if I must die, this old love will too... eventually.
Behind screen I hid my heart but it was useless,
desire for you tore it away now heart all can see!
"Such a demanding love!" My honour complains.
You are either my greatest gift, or worst enemy!

Remembering her, wears away my flesh… bones go,

like a knife carving away at wood, to an arrow make!

It amazes me the story of 'Urwa the 'Udhrite's told

tribe to tribe: he died peacefully, death daily, I take!

Like wine, is the beauty of that one…

and, her clear saliva is like pure wine!

In her, three kinds of wines combine,

each, more intoxicating… more fine!

After dawn has broken, after night has come,

of a beautiful and pure maiden I'm dreaming.

One, loving, slim; but, a curvaceous shape…

full breasts, small waist, like a mare moving.

Neck of a gazelle, eyes like a buffalo's, large:

legs strong like iron, like a river shimmering!

With breast and stomach like a sand dune…

arms branches, grapes, juice, sweet smelling.

Eyes that move direct to hit hearts of all men;

their darts that kill not a one can be avoiding.

In my heart that one has sown love's seeds…

with water of desire, her eyes were watering.

She knows how to strike at this fearful heart:

with a graceful, sleepy dart, make-up hiding.

This lovely woman can make the lover bleed

without feeling guilty… or any price paying.

God… that one could violently kill her lover

without of being brought to justice, fearing;

because, when it comes to the game of love,

was there a time… justice was intervening?

Friend... if you take my greeting to that one,

laid low from grief she will burst out crying:

that worried heart and the veiled love in it,

because of a word from me will be showing!

She will try, but they will like rivers flow...

she'll not be made happy again by anything.

Dawn comes, sun rises... a greeting I send:

sign of dawn is how it you will be knowing!

As the sun rise ten times I'm greeting you:

ten with its shining... ten with its setting!

She asked me, "Why, why insane have you become?"

I answered her, "Love is worse than an insane brain!"

The one who truly loves… that one never gets over it,

while madman's raving only when having fit. Insane!

I believe that this passion… this love that for her I have
will drive me to the wilds: no goods, no mother or father;
without one to turn to, to give a last will and testament,
with only horse and saddle as friends, my lament to hear.
All previous loves I had, by my love for her, are eclipsed,
and it's now more important than all… that went before.

That one is an unhappy one who in the evening is robbed
of his reason, and goes completely insane in the morning.
I am abandoned by my friends, except for those that say
that I'm mad and those who laugh but away are staying.
When again I hear Layla's name then I know once again,
and... a new strength again into my sick brain is coming.

I keep trying to go to sleep but to me sleep won't come

because I am hoping that a vision of your face I'll see!

When I come intending to talk about you, I run away

so I'll be alone, so in secret I can let feelings go of me.

When I come, it's not words about another to listen:

for other than you, I've no interest, not in any other.

I look at who questions me... he thinks I understand:

but, inside my mind is only you; he, does not matter.

O dove of the forest... why, why do you continue to cry?

Is the one you love far off or to torment you is she trying?

When you are singing happily at morning on the branch,

is it passion and desire, that are cause... of your singing?

Lord, make that love of hers the same as mine,

so neither I nor Layla an advantage are having.

Or else, make it I find her hateful, and her kin:

Lord of the Throne, this, a gift I'd be receiving.

O you gazelles of her encampment, where have you gone
with my Layla, when all stars in the sky have appeared?
The camp of Layla is at al-Mathaba, and around it birds
moan, cry and coo for outside her tent is always deserted.
My heart beats painfully with love and desire to see her:
how can this youthful passion of mine be ever appeased?
Shouldn't I follow Layla immediately to where she went,
to where she pitched her tent? People meet... are parted!
And... if this body of mine is lying far away from yours,
then in truth... Fate, my heart to yours, has been joined.
I'm a stranger in love, full of longing outside your tent...
outside a strange dwelling every one feels down-hearted.
Once again Destiny has dealt a heavy blow to my heart:
once again... this victim, by her lack of constancy is led.
O my Layla, it was only ever your glances satisfying me!
Only one satisfied by glances knows love... this is said!
Look at me! I go and go to sleep in the middle of the road,
like an owl's brother... whose wings have been fractured.

From their riverbed the torrents came rushing down…
from my eyes a great flow of tears they were drawing;
because I am knowing that to a far place their waters
are going, to a valley… its way to your feet, winding.
Now, they're bitter as they are passing: going to you
they flow and become sweet, with your scent playing.
When I am walking among all my kinfolk, I'm alone…
they are avoiding me but strangers they're welcoming.
If one is travelling to the south of Hima there is a hill
that stands there that I love, but near I'm never going.
What is worth of a world where one's love is far off…
and not one is getting up, to you home be welcoming?

It was on the pilgrimage day, that I last saw Layla...
at Mina in Mecca's valley, with stones everywhere.
And every time she lifted the sleeve of her long tunic,
she revealed a beautiful arm, fine red markings, there.
When dawn came up it found me rooted to that spot,
on star in the west as it dropped, these eyes did stare.
How fortunate was this one who has lost his mind...
a mind that left me and left here, there... everywhere.
I am deserted by old friends I trusted... I excuse them,
although they still criticise me... when I am not there.
When I hear Layla's name mentioned, mind returns...
like horses come back from galloping off... somewhere.
Then they are saying, "That one's now normal, not a
trace of madness exists, he is just one who does stare,
talks strangely; thinks he loves, but her... cannot see!"
No, they don't know what it is: before anything there
was love, I did bear... and revealing this are all of my
tears... and my flesh, that from limb to limb is spare;
and, O my Layla, there is now nothing remaining but
the echoes that on the wind that flies past, go to her!

O twin mountains of Numan, allow that breeze
to blow freely, so its breath will reach me purely,
so, that I can find its freshness… or, it may cure
the burning fever that consumes my liver totally.
Anyone inhaling that soft breeze from the east
is able to make peace with his soul… in agony!
As long periods went by Numan welcomed us:
after we'd pitched camp our tribe played freely.
O breeze, flow past that camp and let me know
if there are traces, or are they gone, completely.
O Layla, this illness that I have is so ancient:
pain of love, going on so long, is more deadly!
Etched in this mind is the mornings we met…
a white she-camel I rode to see you so proudly.
Way back then all life was a beautiful thing…
we never knew any grief as we were so happy!
Layla's why my eyes are now weak from tears:
pouring, the wound in them is for an eternity.
O friends of mine, this bleeding heart cover…
because in no time at all, it just ashes will be.

Layla's heart's is being poisoned by their lies:

if she thinks of me I forgive all her unfairness.

Layla, heart never hates or wants to leave you,

although you've given me not much joyfulness.

Many times, some kind being upon seeing me,

shouts, "Look, Layla's worshiper, in distress!"

That one's my eye's freshness when nearby...

if they turn on her, I love her with a madness.

Time and again they say... "To God repent,"

but I don't... I need her so! I'll never confess!

Tears started to flow when I saw Mount Taubad
and as it saw me, it... "God is great!" exclaimed;
upon seeing it I shed tears, it called loudly to me!
I said, "All them and I, around you awhile lived!"
It replied, "They went off, left the country to me:
is anyone left in one place by life that's troubled?"
I cry from fear you'll leave me soon, as our camps
were once joined: now, my tears are a great flood!

This longing of mine takes me to Layla's land...
to scold her for this love that causes such agony.
On the earth, my eyelids like clouds pour rain...
this heart of mine's eaten up by pain and worry.
To the camping-ground I reveal my great grief,
and like some river my tears are flowing freely.
In the sand I go on drawing you, to talk to you:
can this earth hear my prayers... any possibly?
I go on imagining that I'm near you, but... no,
this talking and weeping the earth hears, only.
All about me it is silent, no one else is talking:
the one I am complaining to, answers silently.
When all hope has left me these tears of mine
drop like rain, from the clouds... abundantly.
Because of you, I am Majnun... mad for you:
my heart from loving you burns passionately.

O gazelle, so like Layla, do not fear because
today in my wild state I'm your friend, truly.
O gazelle… so like Layla, if you'd only stop
awhile heart would grieve less… believe me.
As I have untied the rope around that one it
takes off: but I do it for Layla… not, for me!

Ah you crow, you are the bird of separation...

your deathly hue brings back time of parting.

When you rest, what do you say? O tell me!

Tell me, when you fly, what are you saying?

And, if what you are telling me is true, your

grief's without end and broken is each wing.

They always hunt you and you aren't saved

like I'm not too... me they keep persecuting!

Let me do this mad wandering that I do...
can't you see this frail body will soon die?
This poor heart of mine has suffered a lot:
fire of longing, torture, beaten by each lie.
Now, too tiny for me is God's great land:
can a safe place for a madman ever apply?
I'm in agony due to separation and desire:
she is so far off union is impossible, say I.
"Where's Layla? They hide her now from
me, who easily found her before?" I sigh.

In a meadow I saw a gazelle, grazing:

in the sunlight I thought it was Layla!

Eat peacefully gazelle, I am a friend...

take your time I am your rock, forever!

When I'm flashing sword it's glowing,

when I'm lunging it's death to deliver!

I saw a wolf the gazelle attack... teeth

and claws in that belly to tear asunder.

With arrow I let fly I struck that wolf...

I saw life leave its throat, like thunder!

My pulse was settling... my anger was

cooling: but, a real man's a true avenger.

Is it possible to soften the pain in this heart?

Death's darts, than your hands, are... closer!

I want much, I lose too much and I am away:

you can't get nearer to me and I'm away, far!

This love of ours is like a tiny bird some boy

ties up that falls into death's pond and there

you are for he continues the game... without

feeling bird's pain... wings without a feather.

A thousand places and paths I'm knowing...

but, unless there is a heart, there is nowhere!

In the place where the moon dips, shine:

as the dawn is now late the sun become!

The light of the sun you are reflecting...

but your smile and lips, has not the sun.

You look like sunlight, moonlight haloed:

but, eyes are too bright, for moon or sun.

The first ray of moon you are shining but

it has not a neck like you... it has, none!

And where are those dark eyes and those

sleepy, hooded lids like yours, of the sun?

Layla, when I'm looking at you my cheek turns pale,

and, O sweet girl, on yours I see a blush get deeper!

Layla, will I tell you why this change is happening?

Crimson stream leaves my heart, your face to cover!

When with the village girls you played they seemed

lovely, but... when you went their beauty did suffer!

For that soft earth of Al-Hidjaz I am longing,

that camping-ground in Najd, I desire to see.*

And yet it's so far, so far off, much too far off

like it's a mirage and to look for Najd is crazy!

Whether right or wrong I go on... late or early.

I'll stay, look! Each day I'll look, I'll cry... see!

Water goes on filling my eyes and overflows:

in this thumping heart when will peace... be?

This heart is full of sadness when she comes,

or when she's far away with longing... crazy!

This is what they keep saying, " Look at him

cry and see how she killed him, completely."

Listen to me: these are no tears that pour out

of my eyes, merely my soul dripping from me!

*Notes: Al-Hidjaz is a province in the Arabian Peninsula that is mountainous and is on the west-central coast. Najd, the place of Layla's family's encampment sometimes, is in central Saudi Arabia and is a rocky plateau that slopes in an eastward direction from al-Hidjaz.

You stripped bones of skin, I don't have any anymore:
in light of sun and cold of night… you left them bare!
These bones no more have any marrow, look and see!
They are like reed pipes… wind blows through there!
You will hear it blowing some day and then… afraid,
you'll remember the one who loves you, who is here.
Then, in that mixed-up soul of yours, your fear will
make those inhibitions of yours, quickly disappear!
Come here now and by my hand be pulling me up:
look closely at me and see what you've done, here!
Ah no, I'll hide this destitution that I am feeling…
if you are not merciful I'll still not leave you, ever!
God… I did all I could to make her find happiness.
I'm just a loving man, unfaithful to You I declare!
What pours out of my eyes aren't tears one sees…
but, a soul that bit by bit drips out, do You hear?

Wretched madman! I think about my heart stolen

by a love that is impossible, that can't be helped!

This love and yearning that for her I keep feeling

have captured my heart and in it they've stayed.

That man now sharing her life is most blessed...

from anxieties and sorrow him God has spared.

But when I read again the letters that she sent,

all I can do is weep at every word, that she said.

I go telling heart to run from her, it says it will:

but, when I try my longing is far greater made.

My love for this being can't be stopped by me:

torment in my heart by this love is intensified!

All those she hates I'd have mostly agreed to...

heart, drunk on her, would not have consented.

More one tries to stop passion, more it grows:

fruit that's forbidden, more it becomes desired!

If my messages can be sent to Layla, do it fast:

death is soon here! Am I alive... or have I died?

This impatient heart, finds it all too difficult...

it goes on beating, crying, "How hard I tried!"

You... to journey through the night, you made me:
when the grey partridge over Jilhatan is sleeping.
It is many a river that I've been weeping for you:
you who have with anger my heart been breaking.
All my family and others you have set against me,
out of resentment me away they've been sending!
You broke promises... made me an amusing thing
for all of those who before... were you, criticising.
You made me the victim of those who slander...
so, they set on me: for this, you were not paying.
And if those against me could write on my body
I think that their words they would be repeating.

In that place of safety for all of the animals,

is where folk from everywhere come together.

At al-Hatim, my thoughts on her are set so

much this soul is taking its grief back to her.

This one with matted hair, in Mecca prays

so of sins of Layla God will be the forgiver!

"Hear me, merciful One, give me Layla to

begin with... *then* judge her, do You hear?

If Layla's given me while I live, none for a

sin repents unless for same I'm a repenter."

She's my eyes fruit when I see her up close,

and when they slander her I love her more!

They go on telling me, "Remember God!"

I won't, she's my desire, I won't forget her!

Layla, my soul didn't hate, want to leave:

heart... patience, separation isn't forever!

During this pilgrimage I didn't beg due to sins I did,

but... to get some help to get together with someone.

You caused me to love that one when I was young...

and now You see... I am still madly, loving that one.

I'm much older, so... give her back, my sanity return:

or, so our love's the same do it, so it can't be undone.

O my Lord, Who is the One Most Compassionate,

You're famous for Your actions... as, the 'Just One'!

Now, here the pilgrims are surrounding me,

in Mecca it is as if all hearts beat, together!

In the middle of all these clamouring people

these thoughts full of inspiration, fly to her!

In this place of pure souls I said this to God:

"Lord I'm here, sins I regret, I'm a repenter!

I love Layla, but... if I cannot see her again

I can't do that, as this heart is hers forever.

What to do, be obedient to You or You will

punish me, to be with You, to give up her?"

To my friends I say this : "That one's the sun:
light is all around that one, but you can't see!"
Then, I was struck in my heart by the wind…
it was breath of that one, scent fresh… lovely!
The end arrives… not knowing consequences,
never waiting, every word escapes me, finally!
Kin now take me away, me they are carrying:
cry, try to save me, sacrifice own lives easily!

I've been told that, "In Iraq, Layla is not well...
you, that one's closest friend, are not affected?"
All those who are ill in Iraq... God cure them,
because for all who are ill there, I am afflicted!
If the truth's that in Iraq is Layla and she's ill,
death's ocean embrace me, let me be drowned!
From here to there I am passing, for I am lost:
then, at morning the way to Layla I've found.
In this heart of mine a fire One lit for Layla...
it like some bolt of lightning instantly spread.
My poor soul cries bitter tears; then... at last
gasp it remembers you and from love is dead!
Sun's wonderful to me that shames the moon:
when striking, it covers up lightning's thread!
Your curls are more black than pitch and face
more radiant than a moon... O one perfected!
I'm O so restless and I'm O so madly in love;
like slave kept in chains so long I've suffered!
This reasonable mind of mine is O so weak...
now all sleep has left me and eyes are opened!
I'm only veins and bones nothing else to see...
body, heart, soul by love for her is destroyed!

Pity me if I die but please do not blame me…

any lost soul one crying over it has deserved.

And so, over my grave engrave these words:

"Her eyes killed this one, a lover now dead!"

Now, I turn to God and I am complaining:

I ask for God's compassion, it's warranted!

I've endured and loved much too much I say!

For Layla my heart's burning, uninterrupted!

O shepherds of the night... please witness how
the subtle time of dawn has me been weakening!
Ah... does that one know what is happening to
one whose heart's captured: not to be releasing?
Somewhere out here, they pitched their tents...
perhaps, after night fell, they away were going?
And, something else I see... why in the hearts
of lovers are the stars hanging... just hanging?
"It's quite probable... that tomorrow Layla of
the Amirites, or even tonight will be leaving!"
These words told to me in the night are like a
partridge in defeated heart's net, squawking!
That one flies bravely, but, wings are caught:
those chicks of that one are in desert... dying!
And then the wind begins to blow with anger
and the nest of that one is falling and falling!
When those chicks hear that wind, cold they
call out, "Mother come back... be returning!"
But, during that night all hope ebbs away...
what is the use, and no help in the morning!
O shepherds of the night, live as you will...
when I could have been a lover I was dying!

As I was looking at the camp, it was like
I was seeing it through shimmering water.
Love caused all to blur as my eyes in tears
that were drowning made me see unclear!
Before when it happened the water went,
then I could see again, it all became clear!
Pouring out of my eyes are not tears this
time but my soul leaking out, is my fear!

Each time that I go to residence of Layla,

must they always my Layla be striking?

When a wolf is lured into a trap like this,

can the lamb be punished for its coming?

Honour Layla, you honour me: hate her...

you hate me! She is soul's joy refreshing!

It's useless to try to stop her greeting me

and to lock her away and on her be spying!

I'll never stay away from Layla... I'll defy

all of those swords held high for cutting:

I will go searching for her throughout the

camp... until her I am eventually finding.

Ah no... if only the joyful fate I want for

Layla, was the destiny I was receiving!

Ah, don't be blaming for risking my life:

beloved of each soul's where to be lying!

O delicate Layla, the ground on which

you are walking, with much love I kiss.

Then, I can hear someone saying, "See

that mad person, who'd act like this?"

It is not the earth I love so I'd kiss it...

I love you and foot that touching it is!

I am truly mad with love for just you:

when I remember us, I feel some bliss!

I've to live in the wild far from others,

in the hope with animals I find peace.

That the camp's in the east isn't its fault,

or... east or south wind dunes blow away!

O these horses, I wish they would all die,

us lovers by them are separated each day!

After dawn, riding off to arrive on time...

without a trace heart is back there a way!

In heart a fire burnt as I went into their country…

then they asked me as they were approaching me:

"You do not seem to be afraid of our lions, why?"

I replied, "With beloved, one's soul wants to be!"

O Layla, we know that out of kindness
and love over me you have been crying.
Strange! We live nearby but are in pain
as we can't each other, ever, be seeing!
The sickness that I am suffering from
is love, and... a desire that is growing!
Layla, such a kind woman as you over
an orphan-slave is most likely crying.
Layla, reason cried bitter tears over me
on seeing what my heart was suffering!

O God... help me, always I think of that one!

Layla, what sin did I commit? I am confused!

O God, I don't know why You have left me!

Layla... to you what did I do? Let it be said!

Do you want us not to see each other again?

It would be so much easier then, to be dead.

The cup no one drinks from, will I empty it:

or, will I just go far away... empty-handed?

The other thing that I could do is reveal all,

but... if I do that I will be lost, not trusted.

Layla, you're so confused in relation to me:

I'm one others stay far from! I'm slandered!

O Layla, listen closely to what I'm saying:

our souls will be uniting, after we're dead!

Earth will not be able to hide us from us...

like birds our souls will meet, uncluttered!

O Layla... this freed soul will be rejoicing

when your fine voice it hears unobstructed!

Then, to these eyes of mine I will say this:

"Keep on, cry without end, tears of blood!"

I can clearly see that love's a fire, aglow...
and, on hearts of lovers itself it is feeding!
It would be alright, if after they had burnt
away they would totally away be passing!
No, when they are ashes, like the damned
they return for new torments experiencing.

By that One who lives over Mt. Thabir*

where the clouds are gathering, I swear,

and... by that old, exhausted camel too,

that through desert gallops with anger:

I have loved Layla for such a long time,

I truly say that my life or death, is her!

*Note: A mountain in Mecca.

In Mecca we removed all the saddles,

because our horses were all exhausted.

I asked a scholar of Islamic law I met:

"She I only think of, will be released?"

He replied... "O no! By God, agonies

without a pardon she will have had!"

I burst into tears that ran on my shirt:

"God, forgive sins, forget she's bad!"

When we were in al-Khaf, in Mina, not knowing
a man shouted a name and renewed soul's agony.
The name he shouted was "Layla"... she wasn't
near... it was like a bird left my heart, suddenly.
That one called "Layla!" God, his eyes tear out!
For she's in Damascus, out in the desert is she!
To my heart I say, "Patience," then, it replies...
"From now on be anxious, but, go on... bravely!
Your beloved has been taken far away from you
and longing for her burns like a coal... slowly!"

It's happened at last, now Layla is mine,

but... only occasionally I can be with her.

When her relatives and tribe come back,

I am not allowed to come anywhere near.

I love Layla and she is such a passion for

me that fate wants to take away forever.

Ah no! Now I have to leave my Layla...

because now the caravan's arrived here.

Now, the kith and kin of Layla are back

any bliss in Layla's love does disappear.

O Layla, twenty years is so long, I'll not leave again:

weeping from anguish, here I will stay, wait for you!

The killer of my ill heart is this love for you I suffer...

what to do to stop a killer, if love is what I must do?

Wherever Layla goes I go too, then she has to leave:

unification, separation... is life we must go through.

Around this heart of mine, I've permitted a chain...

Layla's dragging me along... I am following on cue!

I tremble as my road is surrounded by the darkness

like I was mad, and my limbs knew not what to do!

I woke up, then new agonies became available…
movements of my body were due to love, weaker.
At the Little Bear and the Pleiades I was gazing:
love, it is making even ordinary things… bleaker.
That one whom I love, that rosy-cheeked beauty
is there before me in the sky, a rising star, clear!
I'm mad for you, I love you… I think of no other:
it is only for you, these eyes weep many a river!
My desire was, if you died it was me who died:
that, it'd be one grave that our bodies did bear!

If after death, the lovers were asked this:

"Lovers, of all your agonies are you free?"

They reply, "Truly our bodies are ashes,

but love's fire in hearts burns, brightly.

Eyes of a body in grief, tears drying up:

now in soul's eyes tears flow eternally."

O grave of Layla, if all Arabia's and Persia's women

saw where you were, they'd all scream, in mourning!

O grave of Layla, always be protecting, honourably,

that one who into our life grace was always bringing.

O grave of Layla, that one is now a stranger to all...

there's not a kith or kin by the side of her, standing!

O grave, you have never in the past embraced such

a one as Layla... a fine, pure woman, now reclining.

O you grave of Layla, all of them are now far away:

her mother, auntie, all who her life sought to sway.

O Layla, I recall all days, years that are gone:
bliss that went on and on and heart so happy!
Days, you went by fast, like a lance's shadow
that went by with happiness, her: but not me!
Ah, clearly I can remember Thamdin, with its
fire... Layla, that glowed, so that we did see!
Another time, as my companions spurred our
horses along, to al-Ghada we went, furiously.
A companion with the eyes of a falcon said...
"Towards Yemen a star in night's heart I see!"
Then I shouted, "That fire up there in the sky
is for Layla, and it has shown itself... for me!"
Companions, was it really a necessity to ride
through al-Ghada? Why were we in a hurry?
Ah, if only all these places we went through
during night had taken us to them suddenly!
Layla... so many worries and desires have in
me grown... where are you if night leads me?
Friends, when you're tired of over me crying
I'll find another to weep for me more deeply!
As a young man, I've known great longing...
so now I make up poems to calm my anxiety.

God, at times, brings tragic lovers together,
who did believe that they'd never united be!
God, damn all saying, "Your love, life cured.
Layla long ago brought cattle in… you see?"
All that is hers can grow up… even children:
all that is hers in my heart live permanently.
We once sat in a secluded arbour, but… were
found… now, such places are hateful to me!
O God, give grace to Layla and her friends,
when camped in a far-off valley, one can see.
I'll never forget her, if I'm poor or I'm rich…
if a road leads into her arms, I will be happy!
O women, it is useless to on a beautiful one
put make-up and say, "She is Layla… see!"
O my friends, I have to put up with our fate:
God, breaks hearts, He gives her, not to me.
You say, "In Tayma, Layla's tent is pitched,
all of the summer it's there and she will be!"
I have seen summer speed away, O Layla…
why is road taking you from me so lengthy?
If I live in Hadramawt, in these mountains,
to Yamama comes some slanderer after me!

God damn them, why are they all so joyful
that Layla and I are separated deliberately!
I always wished to of this love be a master:
now, when all has gone, my master I do see!
O let the love between us become one love:
let it stay strong... never, let it change me!
Let the star rise... to that way be showing,
let morning arrive, and my desire, more be!
Out of Damascus I can be far... so far off:
if all folk there Canopus see, it's her I see!
If near me one speaks of some other Layla,
my clothes are wet by my tears so quickly.
If to her country the southern wind blows,
I fall in love with that night wind, nightly!
They watch her; they forbid me to see her?
They, cannot take from me... this poetry!
Layla, before God, I state that I love you!
You own this heart, but me... do you see?
God chose another, gave you to that one...
God decided and gave to me despair only.
Ah Umm Malik, of happy days I dreamt:
my hair greyed, and reason... went crazy!

Every night, I keep counting the nights...
in the past, I lived, not counting nightly!
I am able to leave the camp, and alone at
night I am thinking that you I might see.
Even at prayers I am drawn to see you...
I do not look forward, back... improperly.
I am no infidel, but, this longing for you
awakens grief... doctors cannot help me!
The name that fits me is, the 'loveable':
that is, if yours is similar... my 'lovely'.
Friends, she's my dream, or destruction!
One with me is with her, her... with me!
O pigeon of al-Aqiq I owe you my tears!
You know these tears are for you... only.
O friends, what to expect from this life:
my joy is for sale, bought by... not, me!
Layla hurts me, says, "He, forgets me;"
but, all know my condition, intimately!
When, one thinks of friends or lovers...
we... are perfect, one soul, in each body!
Two friends, with the hope of uniting in
the world? No, but we would like to be!

True, I fear you, afraid to see you again:
I fear it happens, in my dreams you'll be!
I listen to them... "Majnun, from 'Amir
tribe, all he needs is to rest, completely!"
I reply with... "I suffer, so can I do that?
Desire drove me mad, so desperate, see?
If you come near me, you'll be infected!"
Time goes slowly, then death, suddenly!
This name will be carried along by fate...
all will be revealed, everything... finally.
O my eyes joy, when lost in your eyes...
a burning heart rules their tears, clearly!
You decide, if you wish to make my life
hell or if you want to make me... happy!
Because of you I'm a shadow of myself:
all weep for me, if they hate or love me!
Each time I see her, will they hit Layla?
When I see her, they are all... so angry!
Every time I start a journey, I caress my
she camel... lead her to heart's destiny.
If Layla calls me, to the south or east...
wherever, if she waits, I go, eventually!

I want to sleep but sleep does not come:
your spirit will come, to me... possibly?
You are a witch, but... even witchcraft
by powers can at times... defeated, be!
But not when about me, it is all about...
me... who Layla holds in a spell, totally!
And... when I get close to you, night is a
surprise: our horses lead to you... to see!
Heart lets go reins ruled by desire's fire:
O burning heart, that is consuming me!
You riders of Yemen, be resting near us,
in Yemen our beloved's staying nightly.
Tell me later, did Na'man's creek flow;
valley's stream like love flow naturally?
Pigeons of Na'man, such a storm in my
heart woke when you cooed just for me!
One's honour is not hurt if one is alone:
but... before companions I wept bitterly.
Sing pigeons, answer each other's coos,
sing of our meeting at al-Ghada happily.
Layla, will I ever know which white hairs
on my head are due to you, to love, or me?

You they slander, but with no idea about

who they say such evil things… openly.

O Umm Malik, it's said that lovers pass

but the love in one's heart stays eternally.

God, I beg, if You've made Layla my fate,

with my eyes that love her, let her see me.

If not, then let me be free from this desire,

for... having met her has been my tragedy.

Any man, would take his life for a woman

like Layla, even when despair's normality.

O friends, if I am ordered not to meet her,

make death's bed, shroud, ask His mercy!

APPENDIX ONE

Nizami's 'Layla & Majnun'

(From Paul Smith's Translation of Layla & Majnun)

In 1188 Nizami is found to be in happy frame of mind. One day
he received a message, which gave him the opportunity of
setting to work this new energy of his spirit. The king of
neighbouring Shirvan, Abu 'l-Muzzaffar Shirvanshah
Akhsitan, wished him to elaborate the love-story of the
celebrated pair of young Arabian lovers Layla and Majnun.
This king's origin, with whom began a new dynasty for
Shirvan, reached back to the old kingly dynasties of Persia and
so he regarded himself as *the* representative of Persian
nationality and spirit and wished at least to animate his not
very widespread dominion... by making it the protector of
Persian literature. The request of the prince to Nizami had
probably no other ground than to draw to his court from his
quiet seclusion the poet who was already so renowned that he
was able to say of himself...

I have brought to such refinement my enchanting poetry,

my name "The mirror of the world to come" will now be!

The task asked of him by no means at first appealed to Nizami. The subject proposed was indeed a worthy one... as he expressed himself about it...

Love stories... there are more than a thousand,
which by tip of a pen are made into a legend...
however this one is the king of all love-stories:
what can it be, with all artistry that in me lies?

But soon the subject appears to Nizami to be too dry to be turned into a great poem. The desolate Arabian wilderness for his theatre, two simple children of the desert as his heroes, nothing but an unhappy passion... this might well daunt even the poet of 'Khosrau and Shirin', which in everything, place, persons, and treatment, presented the greatest variety and grandeur. He says...

The entrance court of the story is too contracted:
poem would suffer, going backward and forward!
Race-ground of poetry ought to be more spacious
if it's to show off the ability of the rider, I stress.
A verse of Koran may deserve to be well known...
but, a commentary on it may become overblown.
Fascinations of poetry are its joys and flatteries;
from these two sources is derived its harmonies.
On such a journey in which I know not the way,

can I know where are the pleasant spots to stay?

There may be neither gardens nor royal banquets,

nor music, nor wine… not anything, but regrets.

Only rugged mountains and endless arid sands…

until poetry becomes an aversion in one's hands.

But the persuasion of his son Mohammad, at that time fourteen years old and his regard to the prince's request convinced him to overcome his reluctance and he soon began work. Nizami once aroused was able to exhibit an extraordinary activity. Within a short time he completed this master-work of love-poetry, which in the comprehensive laying-out of the plan and the connected execution of the several parts has remained unsurpassed although even such poets as Hatifi and Jami and the great Azerbaijani poet Fuzuli and many others inspired by Nizami's most famous work have at later periods treated the same subject. As to the quickness of the composition, Nizami says…

These four thousand couplets and some more

I wrote in less than months numbering four:

if I'd not been held up by another occupation,

fourteen nights may have seen its completion.

How then was it possible for Nizami to complete this amazing literary masterpiece in such a short time? First he would have had access to the Arabic work of Abulfaraj al-Isfahani (died. 967), the *Kitab al-Aghani,* in which there is a chapter of over ninety pages on the young poet Qays or Majnun ('madman'), the lover of Layla who lived in the second half of the seventh century among the Bani Amir tribe in the Najd desert... a collection of traditions interwoven with verse. Other books earlier contained stories about the young lovers but Nizami's greatest source must have come from the collected poems of Qays Ibn Mulawwah (Majnun) himself.

In his outward circumstances, Nizami's new work led to no change. The invitation from Shirvan could not move him to expose himself to the disagreeable atmosphere of the court. He however used the opportunity to warn himself and others...

Refrain from seeking the society of kings:
like exposing dry cotton to fire's burnings!
Light from the fire may be pleasant enough,
but to be safe one must stay a distance off:
moth that's allured by the flame of a candle
is burnt when a companion at banquet table.

Kizil Arslan's gifts had enabled him to live a quiet country-life. One can discover, among many personal intimations in the introduction to 'Layla and Majnun' that takes up over half the book, no complaint of want and even in the dedication appears no request alluding to it. Tranquilized by his quiet life, he says...

In your village, upon your own private estate,

do not think of eating from the other's plate.

Fortune will turn upon that unthinking fellow

whose foot beyond his garment he will allow.

That bird which flies beyond its own sphere...

measures its own flight with death's measure.

That serpent that's not keeping to its own path

twists itself in its twisting into its own death.

If the fox should begin to fight with the lion...

you know which hand the sword's lying upon.

It is impossible to underestimate the effect of Nizami's 'Layla and Majnun' on the world over the past 800 years. Many poets throughout this period have copied or been influenced by his story of the young lovers. Many Master-Poets besides Attar, Rumi, Sadi, Hafiz and Jami have quoted from him or like him have used the story of the desperate lovers to illustrate how human love can be transformed into divine love through separation and longing.

Paintings by the thousands, songs (even 'modern' ones by singer-songwriters such as Eric Clapton) in the many hundreds have been inspired by Nizami's long poem… also plays (Shauqi's is wonderful), operas, symphonies and films.

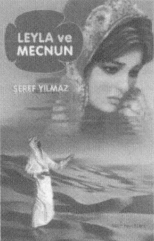

Iran's and perhaps the world's greatest mystical-love poet Hafiz of Shiraz (1320-1392) in his 'Book of the Winebringer' *masnavi* poem, obviously influenced by the one that begins and ends Nizami's 'Layla and Majnun', says...

In wisdom's opinion there's no better adorner of poetry

in this old sphere... than the pearls of speech of Nizami.

Today the influence of his book seems more alive than ever and is growing. Shakespeare's 'Romeo and Juliet' is said to have been written under Nizami's influence (see bibliography).

The Last Sections of Nizami's 'Layla & Majnun'

Now Selim, the generous… who had twice before
sought out his refuge in the wilderness, to implore
the love-sick wanderer to renounce the life he led,
to shun the ruin that was bursting over his head,
once again explored that wilderness… once again
crossed craggy rock, deep valley and dusty plain
to find his new abode. A long month had passed
amongst the wilds… when, turning back, at last
he could see the wretched sufferer this time alone,
stretched upon the ground, his head upon a stone:
Majnun, suddenly looking up, recognized his face,
and told his growling followers to give him space,
then said… "Why are you here again… since you
left me angrily? What now do you wish me to do?
I am a wretch bowed down with the bitterest woe:
doomed, extremes of separation's misery to know,
while you, born into affluence, in pleasure nursed,
a stranger to tragedies… smallest and the worst,
can never be joining, unless in sickening mockery,
such a one who is lost to all of the world… as me!"

Selim replied: "Happily I would change your will,

and take you far away to be your companion still:

wealth shall be yours... peace and all society's joy,

days of tranquility... no suffering will you annoy;

and she... for whom your soul has yearned so long

may still be gained and none shall do you wrong!"

Deeply Majnun sighed, cried: "No more, no more!

Don't speak about the one whose memory I adore,

she whom I loved... held than life itself more dear,

my friend, my angel-bride, my love is buried here!

Dead! But her spirit is now in Paradise, while I...

live... and am dead from grief and yet I don't die.

This... is the fatal spot, my beloved Layla's tomb,

this... is the lamented place of love's martyrdom.

Here lies my life's sole treasure... life's sole trust;

all that was bright in beauty... now gone to dust!"

Selim before him in amazement, paralyzed, stood,

stricken with grief, began weeping tears of blood...

and then some consolation he sadly tried to give.

What consolation... can he make dear Layla live?

Those gentle words and sad looks were only found

to aggravate distraught Majnun's terrible wound,

and after weeks in fruitless sympathy had passed
and his patience still tried, he lingered to the last;
then, with an anxious heart and all hope had left,
that melancholic, tragic scene, reluctantly he left.
The life of Majnun had received the deadly blight,
his troubled day was closing fast, come the night.
He was still weeping... bitter, bitter tears he shed,
groveling in the dust... trembling hands he spread
out... then up in prayer: "God, your servant hear!
And in Your gracious Mercy, free him from here...
from all the afflictions which he must go through,
then in the Prophet's name he can return to You!"
Murmuring like this, on the tomb he laid his head,
and with an exhausted sigh... his weary spirit fled.
And Majnun too... has performed his pilgrimage.
And who ever that exists upon this earthly stage,
who follows the same path? Whatever his claim to
virtue, to honour, to worthy praise, or to blame;
whatsoever he'll answer at that judgment-throne,
where secrets are unveiled, and all things known;
where all deeds of deadly darkness meet the light,
and goodness wears its crown with a glory bright.

Majnun, now removed from this tumultuous scene
which had to him only an unceasing misery been...
at length slept... on the couch his bride possessed,
and on waking, saw her mingled with the blessed.
There, lay stretched out his body for many a day...
protected by his subjects... faithful beasts of prey;
whose presence filled with fear all coming around,
seeking to know where Majnun might be found...
listening... they heard low murmurs on the breeze,
now loud and mournful like the humming of bees;
they still supposed him to be seated in his place...
watched by those wild sentinels of a savage race.
A year had passed, and still their watch they kept,
as if their sovereign was not dead, but only slept;
some had been called away, and some had died...
at last the decayed body was by onlookers spied;
and when the truth had caught the wind of fame,
many old friends from every quarter quickly came:
weeping, they washed his bones, now pure white,
with ceaseless tears all performed the funeral rite,
and... opening the tear-washed gravestone wide,
mournfully... laid him by his beloved Layla's side.

One promise bound their faithful hearts… one bed
of cold earth united them… when they were dead.
Separated in their short life, how cruel their doom!
Never to be joined alive… only in the silent tomb!
The Arabian minstrels legendary songs chronicle
the young lovers tragedy and also delight to dwell
upon their matchless purity… their undying faith,
and how their dust was united, together in death:
it's told… Zayd saw in a dream the radiant bride
Layla with a blissful Majnun, seated side by side.
Zayd one night, dreaming, flashed into his sight…
stretching before him… endless vistas of delight
and experiencing the world of spirits… as he lay,
many glowing angels appeared and there did stay
with many circles of glory around them gleaming,
their eyes with holy rapture towards him beaming
and as he gazed he saw the ever-verdant bowers..
with golden fruit glowing… and blooming flowers;
the nightingales he heard: their sweetness among
their warbling of their rich and melodious song…
and the ring-dove's murmuring and then the swell
of the melody from the harp and the conch shell…

and then... he saw standing in a rose-laden glade,
beneath a wavering palm-tree's extensive shade...
a throne... a throne that was amazing to behold,
all studded with glittering gems, made of gold...
and gorgeous celestial carpets near it were spread,
close to where pure water ran along a river's bed;
and there upon that throne, in their blissful state,
the long-parted lovers... in peaceful love did wait:
resplendent, they sat there in that heavenly light,
and their hands held a cap with diamonds bright;
their lips in turn... his, then hers with nectar wet,
in pure ambrosial kisses met, then met, then met...
sometimes, to the other their thoughts revealing...
each clasping the other with a most tender feeling.
Then... the dreamer who this glorious vision saw,
demanded, with an ever-increasing blinding awe,
what the sacred names were that this happy pair
in this glade of Iram were destined to forever bear.
A voice suddenly replied... "That sparkling moon
is still Layla and her friend is still called Majnun;
as they were deprived in your frail world, of bliss,
they are now reaping their great reward... in this!"

Then Zayd, on waking from his wondrous dream,

thought deeply and long upon its mystical theme,

and later he told to all how those faithful to love

will one day be recompensed by the highest Love.

All of you, who thoughtlessly continue to suppose

that all with worth this flattering world bestows,

reflect today upon just how transient is your stay

here… and how soon even the sorrows fade away!

Ah, the terrible pangs of grief the heart may wring

in life, but Paradise will finally remove the sting…

the world that comes… your happiness will secure

because that world to come is eternal, and is pure.

Ah… what other solace is there for the human soul

but a lasting peace… pure love's unchanging goal!

Winebringer! Now Nizami's poem is finally sung:

this Persian poet's pearls are in the circle strung…

and so, please fill once again this wine goblet high,

and, would you never be asking this imbiber why?

Fill this cup to that love that never changes, never!

Fill this cup to the love that goes on living forever!

To the love that has been purified by earthly woes

and at last with everlasting bliss… divinely glows!

APPENDIX TWO

A Selection of Poetry from the Arabic, Persian, Turkish, Pushtu, Urdu & other Languages, about or Influenced by… Majnun & Layla

(Note: All of the poems below are couplets from longer poems in the forms of the *ghazal, qi'ta, masnavi, qasida*)

SHIBLI (861-946). A pupil and disciple of Junaid of Baghdad and one who had met Mansur Hallaj, Al-Shibli is one of the famous Sufis. He was originally from Khurasan. In the book *Rawdat al-jannat,* and in other biographies, many mystical poems and sayings have been recorded of him. Ansari has said: "The first person to speak in symbols was Dhu al-Nun of Egypt. Then came Junaid and he systematised this science, extended it, and wrote books on it. Al-Shibli, in his turn, took it to the pulpit." He died in 946 at the age of 87. Like Qays (Majnun) he composed his poems in Arabic.

Translation from…

The Divine Wine: A Treasury of Sufi & Dervish Poetry Vol. One, Translations & Introduction by Paul Smith, New Humanity Books, Campbells Creek, 2012.

Majnun declared his love, while I concealed

my passion… so I attained ecstasy's state.

On the Day of Judgement, when lovers are

called to come up, only I will as a lover rate!

RABI'A BALKHI (10th century). Rabi'a is said by 'Attar to have become royalty, her father first becoming king and then her brother. She is the first female poet of Persian whose name and some poems have come down to us. Born in Balkh (now Afghanistan) in the 10th century (although some say Isfahan, others Quzdar) there are many legends about her unhappy love affair. After her father died he put her in charge of her brother Harith. Her love affair was with a slave named Bektash where they sent each other love letters in verse that caused her death when they were overheard by her jealous brother.

Her passionate, gut-wrenching *masnavi* was written in her own blood on the prison walls where she was locked in by her brother until she died. Both 'Attar and Jami state that her love was of a spiritual nature and not physical and she was a highly advanced soul.

Translation from...

Princesses, Sufis, Dervishes, Martyrs and Feminists: Nine Great Women Poets of the East. Translations, Introduction by Paul Smith, New Humanity Books, Campbells Creek, 2011.

It's like Majnun's eyes are from cloud shedding tears,

as him of Layla's cheeks roses are reminding,

in the garden.

All of the dewdrops that in the tulips are collected are

the wine in the ruby cups always resembling...

in the garden.

BABA TAHIR (d.1020). Called 'The Naked', Baba Tahir was a great God-intoxicated soul /mast/ and possibly a *Qutub* (Perfect Master) who composed about 60 known *ruba'i* in a simpler metre than the usual *'hazaj'* metre. His simple, mystical poems that he would sing while wandering naked throughout the land had a profound influence on Sufis and dervishes and other *ruba'i* composers that followed him, especially Abu Said.

Translation from…

Ruba'iyat of Baba Tahir, Translation & Introduction by Paul Smith, New Humanity Books, Campbells Creek, 2010.

> For love to be sweet, it must go both ways…
>
> unrequited love makes a heart, sick… always.
>
> If heart of Majnun for love desperately prays,
>
> the heart of Layla more desperation displays.

*

ABU SA'ID (968-1049) was a Perfect Master and a poet who lived in Nishapur and composed only *ruba'is,* over 400 of them. He was one of the founders of Persian Sufi and Dervish poetry and a major influence on the *ruba'i* and most poets that followed, especially Sana'i, Nizami, 'Attar and Rumi.

Translation from…

Ruba'iyat of Abu Sa'id. Translation & Introduction by Paul Smith,
New Humanity Books, Campbells Creek 2010.

I'm Your Majnun, Your madman, so a help to me be

drunk in Your love by thinking about You, keep 'me':

each one who is helpless has someone to help them…

I'm Your helpless one, so come and help me, quickly?

O Creator, Your creation is one of diversity…

some like *alif,* others bent like *nun* one can see!

Majnun's thoughts in presence of Your Glory

I think they can't be understood by man, or me!

Sometimes, a comb for Layla's black hair

You are…

and in Majnun's head any madness there

You are:

sometimes, Joseph's beauty in a mirror…

You are;

and fire, of Zulaikha's harvest a burner,

You are.

When, living with me, the Beloved was no
longer,
and coat of my wisdom and insight torn did
appear...
finally Majnun came to offer me sympathy:
witness how far my madness has gone, my
dear.

For Your Majnun forest and mountain were
the same...
your love's mad one says head and foot are
the same.
One who knew Your reality lost his self...
one knowing You, knew he and You, were
the same.

*

ANSARI (1005-1090). The great mystical poet Khwaja
Abdullah Ansari who passed from this world 1089 in Herat is
most famous for his biographical dictionary on saints and Sufi
masters and his much loved collection of inspiring prayers, the
Munajat. His *ruba'is* appear throughout his works.

Translation from…

*Ansari: Selected Poems, Translation & Introduction by Paul Smith,
New Humanity Books, Campbells Creek, 2008.
Ruba'iyat of Ansari, Translation & Introduction by Paul Smith,
New Humanity Books, Campbells Creek, 2009.*

If… in the search of the Truth a wanderer

you are,

it's wrong if to the world of secret a teller

you are.

In this Path the heart from anguish will bleed…

Jacob missing son, Majnun missing Layla

you are.

*

FALAKI (1108-1155). Muhammad Falaki was a pupil of Khaqani (to follow) and court-poet of Minuchihr the second, the ruler of Shirwan. 'Falaki' (meaning 'heavenly') was originally an astrologer and gave it up to become a poet. At court under the supervision of Khaqani (a younger man) his talent was eventually recognised and he became a candidate for poet-laureate but unfortunately the king was informed by some rival that he was lacking in loyalty and he was thrown into prison in the fortress of Shabaran. He was eventually released but had become sick and was dead at the age of 47.

Translation from...

Piercing Pearls: The Complete Anthology of Persian Poems Volume One, Translation & Introduction by Paul Smith, New Humanity Books, Campbells Creek, 2005.

That long, curling, serpent-like black hair of yours would hurt

your ruby lip if the narcissus of your eye some spell

casting is not.

Wherever story of your beauty and this love of mine is told...

a wise person about Layla and Majnun's story...

speaking is not.

*

KHAQANI (1122-1199). He was born in Shirwan and died in Tabriz. Khaqani was a great Persian poet and a master of the courtly *qasida.* He was born into the family of a carpenter in Melgem, a village near Shamakhy. He (like Nizami, Sadi and Hafiz, to follow) lost his father at an early age and was brought up by an uncle by the name of Kafi-ud din, a doctor and astronomer at the court of the Shirwanshah, who for seven years (until his death) acted 'as nurse and tutor' to Khaqani. His mother was a Christian of Georgian origin.

Khaqani left a remarkable and large heritage of poems in the Persian language that influenced many of the 'court' and Sufi poets to come, including magnificent *qasidas* with as many as three hundred lines with the same rhyme; lyrical and mystical *ghazals;* romantic, mystical and very personal *ruba'is;*

dramatic poems protesting against oppression, and *ruba'is* and elegies lamenting the death of his children, wife and relatives.

Translation from...

Khaqani: Selected Poems. Translation & Introduction by Paul Smith, New Humanity Books, Campbells Creek, 2012.

> Like the eyes of Khosrau, my luck is sleeping:
> like the lips of Shirin, eyes water are seeping!*
> Like the soul of Majnun my body is in pain...
> like long curls of Layla... my soul is twisting!

*Note: Two other tragic lovers of Persian Poetry and Literature.

*

MU'IN (1141-1230) Muhammad Mu'inuddin Chishti was also known as *Gharib Nawaz* or 'Benefactor of the Poor', he is the most famous Sufi saint and poet of the Chishti Order of the Indian Subcontinent. He introduced and established the order in South Asia. The initial spiritual chain of the Chishti order in India, comprising himself, Bakhtiyar Kaki, Baba Farid and Nizamuddin Auliya (each successive person being the disciple of the previous one), constitutes the great Sufi saints of Indian history.

Translation from...

Mu'in ud-din Chishti: Selected Poems, Translation & Introduction by Paul Smith, New Humanity Books, Campbells Creek, 2012.

If I was burnt in the fire of Your love, is it a wonder?

Mountain Your ray couldn't bear like I willing

do.

Mu'in, Beloved's beauty isn't seen by wisdom's eye:

Layla's beauty with Majnun's eye; such seeing

do!

*

NIZAMI (d. 1208). Born in Ganjeh in Azerbaijhan, Nizami avoided the courts of the various rulers like the plague but dedicated his *masnavis* to a number of them and was paid handsomely for doing so. Often critical of other poets of the time for stealing his verse his high regard for 'the word' and poetry as a spiritually transforming force can be seen below in an excerpt from his first book, the deeply mystical 'The Treasury of the Secrets'... a Sufi classic. His portraits of the various heroines in all of his other *masnavis* (except the Alexander Books) are considered the most profound and influential in all of Persian Literature in relation to women. In his private life his relationships to women were all tragic and had a great bearing on his writing.

A true Master Poet who is most famous for his six books in *masnavi* form: *The Treasury of the Mysteries, Khrosrau and Shirin, Layla and Majnun, The Seven Portraits* (another Sufi classic) and his two books on Alexander. He also composed a *Divan* of approximately 20,000 couplets in *ghazals* and *ruba'is* and other forms... tragically only 200 couplets survive. His influence on 'Attar, Rumi, Sadi, Hafiz and Jami and all others that followed cannot be overestimated. The following is one of his *ghazals*.

Translation from...

Layla & Majnun by Nizami. Translation & Introduction by Paul Smith. New Humanity Books, Campbells Creek 2004/2008.

You keep asking how I am, what do you think, my friend?

My liver is in agony... heart, blood does drink, my friend.

You just be leaving this telling of the story of love to me:

you just be Layla, for I'm Majnun on the brink my friend!

Every day that arrives I keep crying and crying for you...

each day my crying out sounds louder, I think, my friend.

I have heard this... that you are being kind to your lovers:

am I outside Your lovers' circle or on the brink my friend?

Didn't you say if I fell down your hand would help me up:

are you wanting me to fall and to forever sink, my friend?

I was reading some of the *ghazals* of Nizami for you, but,

his charm doesn't have an effect on you I think, my friend!

*

•

'ATTAR (d. 1230). Farid al-din 'Attar is the Perfect Master Poet who was the author of over forty books of poetry and prose including *The Conference of the Birds, The Book of God,* and *The Lives of the Saints.* Apart from his many books in *masnavi* form he also composed many hundreds of mystical *ghazals* and *ruba'is.* He also changed the evolution of the *ruba'i* form by composing a long Sufi epic, the *Mukhtar-nama,* where each *ruba'i* is connected to the one before, something which Fitzgerald attempted to do with those he attributed to Omar Khayyam over six hundred years later.

He was killed by the Mongol invaders outside the gates of Nishapur when at over a hundred years old he advanced on them alone, sword in hand. It is said that after his head was cut off he kept on fighting. In his masterpiece long *masnavi* poem *Ilahi-nama,* 'Book of God, that was to influence Jalal-al-Din Rumi in the composing of his six book masterpiece *Masnavi...* tells a number of stories about the lovers Majnun & Layla to illustrate spiritual points (see following).

Translation from...

Ruba'iyat of 'Attar. Translation & Introduction by Paul Smith, New Humanity Books, Campbells Creek, 2009.
'Attar: Selected Poetry. Translation, Introduction & Notes by Paul Smith, New Humanity Books, Campbells Creek, 2010.

There was a dervish who asked Majnun, "How old are

you?"

That mad one replied... "A thousand and forty years is

true!"

The dervish: "What is that, stupid? You're getting crazier,

dummy?"

Majnun: "One supreme moment Layla showed her face to

me…

I've lived a worthless forty years but it's worth a thousand

years.

Being by myself all those years I was poor in life's coin those

years.

But… that one supreme moment, to a thousand years was

equal

for in being with Layla time beyond measure into my life

fell."

*

AUHAD UD-DIN KERMANI (1164-1238). Auhad ud-din was influenced by 'Attar, Ibn 'Arabi (whom he knew) and Suhrawadi and was a powerful speaker and a Sufi Master whose disciples at one time numbered over 70,000. He used the *ruba'i* form (composing over 1700) in his teaching although he also composed in other forms. Among his disciples was Auhadi of Maragha who took his *takhallus* or pen-name from his master. His ideas and behaviour were said to have shocked many of his fellow Sufis and contemporaries.

Translation from…

Ruba'iyat of Auhad ud-din, Translation & Introduction by Paul Smith, New Humanity Books, Campbells Creek, 2006.

I am Your Majnun, crazily Yours, hold my hand:

You have to know I'm only Yours; hold my hand.

All others who have gone mad have one to help...

I'm mad for You, or madly Yours: hold my hand!

*

IBN 'ARABI (1165-1240). His full name was Abu abd-Allah Muhammad ibn-Ali ibn Muhammad ibn al-'Arabi. In the West, he is also known as the *Doctor Maximus* and in the Islamic world as *Muhyi id-Din* (Reviver of religion) and *al-Shaykh al-Akbar* (Great Master.) Ibn Arabi was born in Murcia in Andalusia, Spain, and his family moved to Seville when he was eight years old. At the age of thirty-five, he left Spain for good, intending to make the *hajj* to Mecca. He lived near Mecca for three years, where he completed his most influential book of poems and began writing his *Al-Futuhat al-Makkiyya* (*The Meccan Illuminations*). In 1204 he left Mecca for Anatolia with Majd-al-Din Is'haq (Isaac), whose son Sadr-al-Din Qunawi (1210-1274) would be his most influential disciple. He finished his influential and controversial book of poems *Tarjuman Al-Ashwaq*, (*Interpreter of Ardent Desires*) in 1215. A vastly prolific writer, Ibn Arabi is generally known as the prime exponent of the idea later known as the 'Unity of Being' although he did not use this term in his writings.

Translation from...

Ibn 'Arabi: Selected Poems, Translation & Introduction by Paul Smith, New Humanity Books, Campbells Creek, 2012.

The religion of Love is what I follow: whatever way

Love's camels travel is my religion, the faith of me!

Examples... Bishr, the lover of Hind and her sister;

Mayya and Ghayan, Qays and Layla... obviously.

*

IBN AL-FARID (1182-1235). Umar ibn al-Farid often called the greatest mystical poet in the history of Arabic literature. His father migrated from his native Hama in Syria to Cairo, where Ibn al-Farid was born and where he lived and died.

The *Divan* of Ibn al-Farid is slim, and the poems in it are of varying lengths. Dominated by the theme of love, they are couched in a beautiful style of great tenderness and sensitivity in which the sounds, patterns, and rhetorical conceits of the language are natural elements of the moods and ideas they convey. Capable of being read as love lyrics, they are intended to be expressions of mystical yearning for God. Almost half of the *Divan* is occupied by a single *qasida* of 761 couplets entitled *Poem of the Sufi's Way*. Considered Ibn al-Farid's masterpiece, this *qasida* is unique in its description of the mystic's experience of God and of the harmony achieved through realising the union of phenomenal existence and pure Being. It has intrigued subsequent generations of Sufis.

Translation from...

Ibn al-Farid: Wine & The Mystic's Way, Translation, Introduction & Notes by Paul Smith, New Humanity Books, Campbells Creek, 2009.

Was it lightning flashing, lighting the spotted mountain...
or, am I seeing flickering in the hills of Najd, some lantern?
Or is it Layla of the Banu 'Amir who at night unveiled her
face and changed the dusk of evening into a shining dawn?

For each man who is charming and every lovely woman are
like that... because Her beauty and charm She was lending.
She made Qays mad for Lubna;* yes, and every other lover,
like Layla's Majnun or 'Azza's Kuthayyir: mad from loving.*
Every one of them was desiring, ardently, that attribute that
She clothed in a form of beauty, in a beautiful form shining.
Because She appeared in physical forms they thought were
some other, while really Herself in there, She was revealing.

*Note: Qays and Lubna, Layla and Majnun, Azza and Kuthayyir... the
names of legendary Arab lovers whose love was never consummated due to
their families not approving of their love for each other.

*

RUMI (1207-1273). Jalal-ud-din Rumi was born in Balkh. He
moved when about eleven with his family away from Balkh so
as to avoid the warlike Mongols. They travelled to Baghdad,
to Mecca on pilgrimage, to Damascus and eventually settled
near Konya in what is now western Turkey.
     On the road to Anatolia, Jalal-ud-din and his father had
encountered one of the most famous mystic Persian poets,

Farid al-din 'Attar (see above), in the city of Nishapur. 'Attar immediately recognised the boy's spiritual status.

For nine years, Rumi practiced Sufism as a disciple of his father Burhan-ud-din until his father died in 1240. During this period Rumi travelled to Damascus and is said to have spent four years there. While there he first caught a glimpse of the *Qutub* (Perfect Master) Shams-e Tabriz. Rumi's love and his great longing for Shams found expression in music, dance, songs and poems in his collection of poems/songs or *Divan* which he named after his Master... *Divan of Shams-e Tabriz*. This vast work included thousands of *ghazals* and other poetic forms and nearly two thousand *ruba'is* that he would compose for many years, before he became a God-realised Perfect Master. Rumi's disciple Hesam'odin Hasan urged Rumi to write the *'Masnavi'* in the style of Sana'i and 'Attar. Rumi completed six books (35,000 couplets) of these before he died.

Translation from...

Rumi: Selected Poems, Translation & Introduction by Paul Smih, New Humanity Books, Campbells Creek, 2009.

Who has ever seen an antidote and a poisoner, like the reed?

Who has seen a sympathetic, a longing lover... like the reed?

The reed, tell of the Path that's full of the bloody stain does;

it, recount the story of Majnun's passion and his pain, does.

The Caliph said to Layla... "Are you really that one who

Majnun became lost and went mad over? That, is... you?

More beautiful than any other beauties... you... are not!"

She replied... "Be quiet! Majnun, one sees... you are not!"

That one who's said to be awake, that one's really sleeping:

much worse than when he is asleep... is when he is waking.

When to Almighty God the soul is not wide awake... of us:

awake is like shutting doors, that One we forsake... of us.

When you let go of your vision and your imagination too...

the candle of union at midnight will be extinguished by you.

In another one he said to... "Snuff it out and do not be driven

to fear the hundred thousand joyful visions you may be given;

for when one snuffs out that candle soul much larger becomes

and your Layla being patient like Majnun, the lover, becomes.

*

SADI (1210-1291). Sadi of Shiraz, a contemporary of Rumi who influenced him, was another Perfect Master Poet who expressed himself in the *ruba'i* form as well as hundreds of *ghazals* in his beautiful *Divan* that often also contained images from dervish dancing.

Sadi was a great traveller who spent forty years on the road throughout the Middle-East, North Africa and India and many of the incidents he experienced he wrote down in his two most famous works when he finally returned to his beloved birth-place... The Rose Garden and The Orchard.

Translations from...

Divan of Sadi. English Version and Introduction by Paul Smith New Humanity Books, Campbells Creek. 2006.
Ruba'iyat of Sadi: English Version by Paul Smith New Humanity Books, Campbells Creek, 2008.

The wise, mere gleaners, know not Layla's secret...

this honour upon harvest-burning Majnun does lay.

Bring others in Your trap, Your slaves we freely are:

bird trained on hand needs not feet tied, in any way.

While his blood kept flowing a lover was saying:

"Soul is in peace, for Beloved a killer of worth is!"

O Sadi, in the opinion of lovers it is all the people

who are insane, while Majnun sane from birth, is!

Each night that Majnun slowly passes after being far away

from his Layla's loving face, is like a night without sunrise.

It's that One's noose that is dragging along the lover's feet:

he never asks how much further in that wilderness still lies.

In whatever direction I was turning my gaze, Your image

was everywhere, like a picture... before my eyes, on show.

When he lay down, the eyes of Majnun only saw Layla...

he would have been a false lover if his eyes sleep did know.

You can't be blamed for the cruel treatment on us falling,

for where from threshold of Layla can Majnun be going?

If I sacrificed my life at Your feet I would never regret it,

for many a life through love and faithfulness is perishing.

What worry should one longing for You have about words?

Nightingale only sings, when rose the garden has entered.

Of what use are the waters of the Euphrates to the thirsty

after death? It wasn't after Majnun died, Layla appeared.

If critic was wise he'd know patience is impossible for Majnun:

he, makes his camel kneel at the place where his Layla will be!

Wisdom's creating many worries that keep wearing out mind:

if you want peace, go away smart-arse: don't be a lover like me!

All Your attributes indicate points of spiritual knowledge:

Your face is demonstrating Divine Omnipotence, I swear!

Don't read the story of the anguish of Layla and Majnun,

Your love has wiped away memory of back then and there!

I don't grieve about Union with You or Your separation...

whatever You order me to do, as Your slave I'll remain so!

O You... more fair than Layla, the fear that I have is that
Your Love will make me, like Majnun... over the hills go!

My story and that of Majnun's are resembling each other:
we have both failed in our quest and died trying, fatefully.
O Sadi, keep on lamenting if you have no way to Union...
the helpless lover has no recourse... but weeping profusely!

It has surpassed the story of Layla's beauty and Majnun's
passion:
if you saw my writing on that One their tale you'd read as
gone!
Sadi's afflicted heart overflows with blood from loving You...
You neither slay him with separation's sword nor give him
Union.

In this love of You our longing and patience are limitless:
heal our mad hearts with Union with You... nothing less!
The ordinary physician doesn't know a cure for lovers pain:
only Layla can cure the anguish of her Majnun's madness.

The bright lightening has flashed and the spring breeze blown,
Majnun's strength's gone... "Where is Layla's tent, confess!"

In opinion of philosophers it's a mistake to neglect love's days.
Dawn breaks, wake up! End of world is annihilation... no less!

A thousand Laylas, a thousand Majnuns could never better

the story of Your beauty or the story of my love, I have been

telling!
Sadi resembles aloes in that until someone happens to burn it

people will not for a moment the sweetness of its perfume find

refreshing.

Many heads strike door like a knocker out of desire:

see whom Fate opening Beloved's door to is drawn.

I fear Layla will perhaps treat her Majnun unkindly

'til the blood of his heart out from his eyes is drawn.

Surely my Layla does not realise that without her beautiful

face the wide world to this Majnun would seem incomplete!

Alas that I didn't realise the value of the time of happiness...

you know Union's worth, when separation you does deplete.

If that Sweetheart I know was to show such a face to others...

theologian would dance ecstatically, preacher drunk would

become!

I'm so drunk you'd imagine there's no hope to be sober again:

Majnun would have become sane again if he'd only wine to

overcome!

*

'IRAQI (1213-1289) Fakhr ud-din Ibrahim 'Iraqi was the author
of a *Divan* of spiritual *ghazals* and *ruba'is* and of the famous
work in prose and poetry *Lama'at,* 'Divine Flashes'… a work
that beautifully describes the mysteries of Divine Union and
became a classic of Sufi Mysticism. He was born in Hamadan
in west Persia and as a child learnt the *Koran* by heart. He
travelled from Persia to Multan in India with a party of
kalandar dervishes where he stayed for 25 years with his
Spiritual Master Baha' ud-din Zakariyya and eventually his
Master made him his successor and after the other disciples
complained about this he left for Mecca and Konya. His grave
is in Damascus beside that of another great Arabian Perfect
Master and poet Ibn al-'Arabi. When seeing these graves side
by side a pilgrim once stated, "That ('Iraqi) is the Persian Gulf
and this is the Arabian Sea."

Translation from…

'Iraqi: Selected Poems, Translation & Introduction by Paul Smith,
New Humanity Books, Campbells Creek, 2010.

From the vault of wine it poured on earth a little,

and in Adam and in Eve a need to express,

stuck.

Into the palm of Layla it placed Majnun's mind:

it, into lip of Azra, Vamaq's soul, no less,

stuck!*

The desire that Farhad strived to fulfil and we're

all alike, in Shirin's sugar-chewing lips, is

stuck.*

*Note: All famous lovers in Persian history and poetry.

The Master: "Silent! Seeing beauty is good for one's eye:

if not I could be Gabriel, that rider soon to fall from sky."

Drunk lovers drink from desire's cup... those only seeing

outer do not know soul: see Layla with Majnun's being!

*

YUNUS EMRE (d. 1321). Yunus Emre is considered by many
to be one of the most important Turkish poets excising a great
influence on Turkish literature from his own time until the
present. He is one of the first known poets to have composed in
Turkish of his own age and region rather than in Persian or
Arabic, his diction remains very close to the popular speech of
his contemporaries in Central and Western Anatolia. Little
can be said for certain of his life other than that he was a Sufi
dervish of Anatolia. His poetry expresses a deep personal
mysticism and humanism and love for God.

He was a contemporary of Rumi, who lived in the same
region. Rumi composed his collection of stories and songs for a
well-educated urban circle of Sufis, writing primarily in the

148

literary language of Persian. Yunus Emre, on the other hand, traveled and taught among the rural poor, singing his songs in the Turkish language of the common people. A story is told of a meeting between the two great souls: Rumi asked Yunus Emre what he thought of his great work the *Masnavi*. Yunus Emre said, "Excellent, excellent! But I would have done it differently." Surprised, Rumi asked how. Yunus replied, "I would have written, 'I came from the eternal, clothed myself in flesh, and took the name Yunus.'" That story perfectly illustrates Yunus Emre's simple, direct approach that has made him so beloved. Interestingly, the name Yunus means 'dolphin' in Turkish.

Translations from...

Yunus Emre: Selected Poems, Translation & Introduction by Paul Smith, New Humanity Books, Campbells Creek, 2010.

Let me sip love's wine again, like Mejnun live in the wild:

night and day love for You... me, keeps holding!

The One I desire!

My name is Yunus the dervish; days pass, my fire grows...

my desire in both worlds is one: One I'm wanting,

the One I desire!

It is wonderful to have such waves as the sea...

a sea deep inside a drop that is infinite, unseen.

Mejnun changed a poem's rhyme with "Leyla":

Leyla and Mejnun who loved her... I have been.

I continue to walk like Mejnun, dreaming of my Beloved:
when I wake up I'm crushed that Beloved I don't see,
see what love did to me?
Wretched Yunus is now lost, wounded from head to feet:
I am far from the homes of those who were friendly,
see what love did to me!

Knowledge increases by words of spiritual adepts.
All not grieving I'd like to send off from assembly.
I'm Leyla; madly in love with Your mercy, Mejnun:
I'd like to be Mejnun so as Leyla's face I could see!

Sufis need parties to talk; others, next world:
Mejnuns need their Leylas… obviously.
It's You I need, You!
If they kill me and toss my ashes to the sky,
my dust would declare there… loudly:
"It's You I need, You!"

Let me sip love's wine again, like Mejnun live in the wild:
night and day love for You… me, keeps holding!
The One I desire!

My name is Yunus the dervish; days pass, my fire grows…

my desire in both worlds is one: One I'm wanting,

the One I desire!

*

AMIR KHUSRAU (1253-1324). The 'Parrot of India' was born at Patigali near the Ganges in India, his father originally a Turk from Khurasan, had fled from the Mongols to India to become an officer in the army in Delhi after marrying a local woman, the daughter of an Indian nobleman. Khusrau states about his remarkable poetic abilities as a boy, "I was then eight years old, but in my swift poetic flights I trod upon the celestial spheres. In that tender age when my milk-teeth were falling, I composed couplets that dropped from my mouth like bright pearls."

Like Nizami, Sadi and Hafiz he lost his father at the age of seven but through his poetic genius and his family's respected position he managed to become a court-poet under Balban of Delhi who took a liking to the young poet and brought him on a number of his military excursions. After the Mongols invaded and killed his patron, Khusrau was imprisoned in 1285. He eventually escaped and returned to Delhi and his mother and a new ruler, Kai-Kobad, who immediately favoured him with his patronage. At thirty-six he was made poet-laureate, serving sultan after sultan.

He was not only fluent in Persian, in which he composed the majority of his many books, but also in Arabic, Hindavi (later known as Urdu) and Sanskrit. Nizami was the major influence upon him and he composed ten long *masnavi* poems in emulation of Nizami's famous *Khamsa*… including his versions of *Layla and Majnun, Khusrau and Shirin, The Alexander Books* and *The Treasury of the Mysteries.* He also composed five *Divans* of *ghazals* and other poems each representing a different period of his lifetime from youth to old age.

In addition to being a Master poet he was also like Rudaki a Master musician who composed music from his childhood days onward, mastering the art of Indian music and eventually perfecting it. He is said to have invented the *sitar.*

His fame spread into Persia and the great Sadi was so impressed with his poetry he recommended he enter the court of Prince Muhammad rather than himself, but Khusraw turned him down preferring to stay where he could be close to his spiritual guide the great Sufi Master Nizam ud-din Auliya of the Chistiyya order. Soon Khusraw became his closest disciple and eventually a Master himself. His poetry reflected his status as a Sufi Master. He rebelled against narrow spirituality and helped to redefine the true Sufi way. He also composed three works in prose.

He was a profound influence upon Hafiz and a manuscript of his poems written by Hafiz still exists in a library in Tashkent. He is seen as the link between Sadi and Hafiz in the revolutionising of the form and involutionising of the content of the *ghazal* and the eroticising of it.

Translations from...

Amir Khusrau: Selected Poems, Translation & Introduction by Paul Smith, New Humanity Books, Campbells Creek, 2009.

Sound of Majnun's chains is for lovers a kind of music

that all who have not loved, have no ear to have heard.

O destiny that turns on me, I've enemies everywhere:
what need for the backstabbers when one is executed?

The barrel's empty but my thirst for wine is remaining:
O heart, drink your blood, if pure wine you're wanting.
Majnun's rattling chain is the music that lovers hear:
ears of the wise such music cannot ever be appreciating.

(Amir Khusraw from his version of 'Layla and Majnun'
On the death of Majnun)

The narrator of this story will now be telling
how Layla, after death, her lover was taking.
The mother of Layla bitterly cried, when she
realized that her daughter had died suddenly.
She tore at her hair that was strewn upon her
daughter's corpse... like the camphor flower.
Most of their friends and relations also were
there and they wept out of grief and despair.
Among them was Majnun, who, on hearing
of her illness had come to the house inquiring
as to how she was doing, he was so dejected.
He heard the sound of crying while he stood

153

outside and he then saw the funeral followed
by the mourners who all full of grief followed.
Seeing the funeral suddenly changed Majnun:
he rushed forward towards it, all of a sudden!
He walked out before it and he began dancing,
he was in a state of joyful ecstasy and singing:
"God be praised for this day... that I am freed
from the torture of separation and am blessed
with such a close union that there is no place
left for body or place, between us... no place!
Salvation I've found, to others not obliged...
I revel in my love, can no longer be criticized.
Face to face we will lie in the same chamber,
arm in arm in a bed we'll sleep, me with her.
From sleep that human sounds cannot wake
I'll not raise head until Resurrection's Wake.
With the pure soul the pure soul will be flying
and with this dust that dust will be mingling.
Be making our grave as small as possible... so
with our bodies squeezed together, we will go.
And, I don't need to feel the grave's closeness
as immortality's garden's beyond more or less."
When the procession did reach the graveyard...

she was in the newly dug grave, carefully laid.
When they were preparing to close it forever…
Majnun rushed from the crowd, O mad lover!
He jumped into the grave and lifted her body:
him press it to his face and chest they did see.
This was too much for the dead girl's relatives,
some leapt into the grave drawing their knives.
Twisting his neck, his lips away from her body
they drew; but, them his dead eyes did not see.
They shook him but there was no life in there…
his body joined hers, his soul flew off with her.
Arm he had put around her wouldn't straighten
and they wanted to separate both of them, then
some old, experienced men warned against it…
saying, "This is a symbol of a divine mystery, it
isn't a human passion, for who for a mere desire
would give up life? In life they never let the fire
of passion control them and in death their purity
is clear to all, and so, don't let the responsibility
of it be on our heads and don't in death separate
those whose souls love joined, never to separate."
And, so the closed the grave above the two lovers,
and to their homes they returned, those mourners.

OBEYD ZAKANI (1300-1371) Persia's greatest satirist and social commentator of the classical period (some say of all time) he was most likely a teacher and friend of Hafiz and a strong influence upon him, and possibly a lover of Jahan Khatun. After moving from the court at Baghdad he spent many years in Shiraz as a court poet and jester. His masterpiece epic qasida *Cat and Mouse* is still fresh and his ribald and outright obscene stories and *ruba'is* are still frowned upon by authorities in Iran. His dervish *ghazals* and *ruba'is* are now considered to be some of the most profound and revolutionary for the period. He was exiled from Shiraz as a result of his criticism of the dictator Mubariz Muzaffar.

Translation from…

Obeyd Zakani: The Dervish Joker. A Selection of his Poetry, Prose, Satire, Jokes and Ribaldry. Translation and Introduction by Paul Smith New Humanity Books 2006.

From : 'The Ethics of the Nobles'

And that other helpless lover who was called Majnun of the

Bani Amir tribe was in the beginning a knowledgeable and

sensible youth but suddenly the love for a girl named Layla

struck him. Out of faithfulness towards her all life became

nothing but bitterness and he never got to enjoy her.

Running naked through the desert he would sing out…

If I happen to be discovering Layla all by herself,

making Hajj to Mecca, barefooted, goes myself.

HAFIZ (1320-1392). Persia's greatest exponent of the *ghazal* and many believe the greatest poet of all time. Shams-ud-din Mohammed (Hafiz), ugly and small, became a God-Realized Perfect Master *(Qutub)*, was twice exiled from his beloved Shiraz for his criticism of rulers and false Sufi masters (such as Shaikh Ali Kolah) and the hypocritical clergy. He was by far the greatest influence on the poets of his time including Obeyd Zakani (possibly his former teacher). His most gifted student, Jahan Khatun (to follow), composed many *ghazals* based on his and praised him in a number of them.

He has been one of the greatest influences in every way on poets, mystics, philosophers and artists in both the East and West. (See my chapter on 'Hafiz's Influence on the East and the West' in my *Divan of Hafiz*).

His *Divan* shows he composed in other forms other than the *ghazal* that he perfected... including his famous *masnavis* 'Book of the Winebringer' and 'Book of the Minstrel' and 'The Wild Deer'... as well as *ruba'is* of which about 150 have come down to us. As with his immortal *ghazals,* his *ruba'is* are sometimes mystical and sometimes critical of the hypocrisy of his times. Apart from *ruba'is* and *ghazals* he composed his masterpiece *masnavis, qit'as, qasidas* and a quite wonderful and unique *mukhammas*.

Translations from...

Divan of Hafiz: English Version & Introduction by Paul Smith New Humanity Books 1986. New Humanity Books 2006

> Majnun's time has passed, now it is our turn...
>
> every one gets five days term; five days: yours.
>
> Love's realm for the lover and a corner of joy...
>
> given to me because of fortunate grace, Yours.

With dawn from direction of Layla's dwelling a lightning flash!
No! See what to heartbroken Majnun's harvest, it totally…
has done!
Wineseller, pure wine; no one knows what Writer of Invisible
does to movement of the compass of all Time… or already
has done.

One night Majnun spoke to Layla: "Beloved beyond compare,
to you will appear many lovers, but the one in a mad state
won't go."
O eye, don't try to wash grief's engraving from Hafiz's heart,
it is cut by heart-owner's sword and bloodstains from slate
won't go.

Nights of close friendship count as gifts, for after our time,
sphere turns many times, many nights, days of wakefulness
brings.
Bearer of Layla's burden, whose order is to cradle the moon,
God, maybe that one's heart, direction of Majnun's distress
brings.

Who would try to hold our terrified, runaway heart?
Madman Majnun escaped from chains, give news to.
Hafiz, at this banquet do not tell of your repentance,
or the arrows of Winebringer's glances will strike you.

In path to the dwelling of Layla, on which there are many
dangers,
first step's first condition is that of mad Majnun's design...
you are.
I've shown to you the centre of love... hey, do not make a
mistake!
If you do, then when you look, outside circle of Love's line
you are.

Pen's reed has no tongue to make known the mystery of love:
beyond the power of expression is the explanation of longing.
Tie your heart to Layla's hair and in actions become a Majnun;
for to the lover, words of reason are hurtful and worth nothing.

Take that one who would surrender his life for one drop,
take such a one's life and give him a cup to pay the debt.
As in Banu Amir, the tribe of Majnun, many will go mad
if coming out from tribe of Hagy another Layla they met.

JAHAN KHATUN (1326-1416?) Daughter of the king of one of Shiraz's most turbulent times... Masud Shah; pupil and lifelong friend of the world's greatest mystical, lyric poet, Hafiz; the object of crazed desire by (among others) Iran's greatest satirist, the outrageous and visionary dervish poet Obeyd Zakani; lover, then wife of womaniser Amin al-Din, a minister of one of Persia's most loved, debauched and tragic rulers... Abu Ishak; imprisoned for twenty years under the Muzaffarids while her young daughter Soltan Bakht mysteriously died, possibly murdered. She was open-minded and scandalous and one of Iran's first feminists... this beautiful and sensuous, petite princess abdicated her royalty twice. She called herself 'a dervish maid' and is one of Iran's greatest poets whose *Divan* is four times larger than Hafiz's and contains 2000 *ghazals* and hundreds of *ruba'is* and *qita's* and a masterpiece *tarji-band* other forms of poetry.

Translations from...

Hafiz's Friend, Jahan Khatun: Persia's Princess Dervish Poet. A Selection of Poems from Her Divan. Translation Paul Smith and Rezvaneh Pashai. New Humanity Books 2006.

Tell me, O where does the heart of my Layla now go?

Jahan is like Majnun, made mad by her disappearing!

O my dear heart, your sweet life has now finished and

there is nothing left for us... but to continue suffering.

Tell me, O where does the heart of my Layla now go?

Jahan is like Majnun, made mad by her disappearing!

O my dear heart, your sweet life has now finished and
there is nothing left for us... but to continue suffering.

My beautiful Layla has been taken from my sight...
I am like Majnun, who from her loss... lost his head.
When snake of separation strikes and my heart hurts,
do not think it will by a thousand charms be healed.

Away from You, too much my suffering comes:
I'm sad and world of Jahan, into grieving comes.
This heart of mine has become like Layla's that
away from Majnun... madness coming, comes.

*

KADI BURHAN-UD-DIN (1344-1398). He was born in
Kayseri in Central Anatolia and succeeded his father as a
judge (kadi). In 1381 he became the ruler of Sivas but was killed
in 1398. There is only one copy of his *Divan* and that is in the
British Museum. His poems are sometimes obscure but always
inspired by passionate love and spiritual ecstasy. His *roba'is*
were probably the first ever composed in the Turkish language.
He is now considered one of the great early Turkish Sufi *Divan*
Poets. He also composed *gazels* in Arabic and Persian.

Translation from...

Wine, Blood & Roses: Anthology of Turkish Poets, Translations & introduction by Paul Smith, New Humanity Books, Campbells Creek, 2008.

Once more for that Leyla my heart has become like that of

Mejnun...

once more for that Beloved my tears flood like the waters of

Jeyhun.

Let it become that Beloved's lips tear apart this heart of mine?

I looked closely, I saw that between those two, blood did

run!

*

JAMI (Nov. 7, 1414- Nov. 9, 1492). Considered the last great poet of the Classical Period (9th-15th c.) Mulla Nur al-Din 'Abd al-Rahman ibn Ahmad Jami composed forty-three books but is mostly known for his seven *masnavis* epics greatly influenced by Nizami, including the best of them... *Joseph and Zulaikh* and *Layla and Majnun* and *Salman and Absal* and his mainly prose works *Lawa'ih: A Treatise on Sufism* and *The Beharistan (Abode of Spring)*. He also composed three *Divans* consisting of *ghazals, ruba'is, qasidas, qit'as* and other, mainly mystical, poems... he composed prefaces to each.

Translations from...

Jami: Selected Poems, Translation & Introduction by Paul; Smith, New Humanity Books, Campbells Creek, 2008.

Ah, morning breeze, visit and kiss Najd's hills for me,
Friend's scent from that camp there blows fragrantly.
When longing for union grows... why blame Majnun
for following camel-litters, hoping Layla's he will see.

The candle illuminated itself with that One's fire,
in every home a thousand moths did then expire!
When ray from the Light of that One lit the sun,
out from the water the lotus in response did come.
Layla decorated her face with that One's beauty,
causing Majnun to long... each hair he had to see.

Majnun and Layla are separated by desert that isn't crossed
until Majnun is Layla, Layla is Majnun... that, this...
too!
Jami, only ever talk about the Beloved, because in the middle
of lovers all other things are worthless: merely that, this
too.

It's said Layla and Majnun had a one-way love,
Layla and Majnun to each other confided:
"For you heart trembles."
In this old world that has so many distractions,

the lovers have always told the Beloved...
"For You heart trembles!"

(From Jami's 'Layla and Majnun')

When I withdrew veil from off this mystery
and prepared this strange song for delivery,
parrot of my genius was an eater of sugar...
from my story told, of Joseph and Zulaikh.
In that pouring of sugar there was springing
sweet couplets, that with it were mingling.
From it excitement was hurled on the world
and happiness in hearts of lovers, unfurled.
It was a fountain that was bestowing grace,
but... from it, *my* thirst was still in place.
And so, this bird of my heart was desiring
to sing another song, another tale be telling.
Then, under fortunate auspices I did alight
on one story, a poem upon Majnun's plight.
Even though in times that have passed two
Masters, high in the realm of poetry... too
loosened tongues in subtleties so profound,
by doing so, did full justice to pure sound...

one pouring pearls, a treasury from Ganja,

other scattering sugar, the parrot of India;

one... who smote the ears of all pretension,

one, who unveiled the bride of Idealisation:

one, with his poetry upon a rock engraving,

one... by his exquisite art colour... painting:

one, raised his flag to the zenith of glory...

the other one preparing the spells of sorcery.

I have also bound tight my belt behind me

and seated myself on my fleet dromedary...

and, where ever their Rakhsh* travelled to,

through their inspiration, that is mine... too,

I've also urged my camel on in all humility,

and brought myself into their dust... finally.

Even though I may fall behind their nobility

their dust upon my face is enough... for me.

*Rakhsh was the famous brave horse of Rustom... the Hercules of Persia.
See Firdausi's 'Shah-nama'.

When Dawn of Eternity was whispering, Love,

fire of longing into the Pen was casting... Love.

Pen raised head from the Tablet of Not-Being,

drew a hundred pictures wonderful to be seeing.

All the heavens are truly the offspring of Love...
all elements fell to earth, from... giving of Love.
Without Love are no tokens of evil, or good too:
any thing not of Love does not exist... is untrue.
And, this high azure roof that goes on revolving
through each day and night... onward turning...
it, is the Lotus of the Garden of Love, yes it is...
ball lying in curve of polo-stick of Love, yes it is.
And, the magnetism that in stone was inherent,
which its grasp so firmly on iron it does fasten,
is a Love... that is precipitated in the movement
of iron that has from stone gathered movement.
Look at stone... see how it becomes weightless,
through longing for its opponent, it weighs less:
from this be seeing how those who suffer sorrow
in the longing for those who the heart loves, so!
Even though to Love is O so painful, so hurtful,
it is the consolation of those breasts, pure, full!
Without the blessing of Love how can any being
escape the grief of the inverted wheel's turning?

AMANULLAH (died 1550). Shaikh Amanullah Panipati, a learned Sufi and theologian and resident of Panipat was one of Humayun's chief poets and Amanullah wrote several *qasidas* in praise of his emperor. His style is comparatively simple and his poetry sweet and full of pathos. He was famous in his day for his *qit'as* in the form of chronograms (where the numerical value of the letters of the last line spell out a date, usually of the death of a famous person of the time).

Translation from...

Shimmering Jewels: Anthology of Poetry Under the Reigns of the Mughal Emperors of India (1526-1857), Translation & Introduction by Paul Smith, New Humanity Books, Campbells Creek, 2009.

Like Layla you are living in seclusion of beauty...

I roam world like Majnun, mind gone completely.

Although the soul leaves the body full of remorse,

from heart love for you won't go, even eventually.

*

FUZULI (1494-1556). Fuzuli (pen-name that means 'perfect') was Muhammad ibn Syleyman who is thought to have been born in a small town in the region of Baghdad, Kerbala or Najaf. He moved to Baghdad which he only left in his old age to make a pilgrimage to Kerbala where he died from cholera. His contemporaries called him the 'prince of poets', but he spent his life torn between impossible dreams of travel and glory and a relatively mundane daily routine.

He wrote many *qasidas* in honour of potential patrons, but it is in his intensely mystical *gazels* and other poetic forms in Azeri-Turkish, Persian and Arabic and his masterpiece version of *Leyla and Mejnun* (in *gazels, mesnevis* and *qasidas*) that his great fame rests, like Hafiz (perhaps the greatest influence on him) as a poet who combined successfully the praising and understanding of human and divine love and the fusing of them. In the true Sufi tradition he saw human love as a bridge to the Divine. He also wrote of theology, medicine, ethics and astronomy. A number of *Divans* some 700 *gazels* and a hundred *qasidas* in Azeri-Turkish and Persian, and twelve surviving *qasidas* in Arabic bear witness to his genius that has not diminished over time. See Appendix Four for the famous opera based on his version.

Translation from...

Wine, Blood & Roses: Anthology of Turkish Poets, Translations & introduction by Paul Smith, New Humanity Books, Campbells Creek, 2008.

We are caravan venturing through the fearful track of purity;

it was Mejnun's, now it's my turn, to guard this train of

faithfulness.

Don't think our cries pierce the silent night have no reason...

we're watchmen of Faith's fort in the domain of Love... no

less!

Farhad and Mejnun drank Love's wine and were knocked out:

while they're sleeping, will we Fuzuli, Love's toasting still

express?

[From the beginning of his version of Leyla and Mejnun]

All praise to You, the great giver of generosity;
to the Owner of mercies, my thanks I'm saying!
For You, from Time's beginning, never change,
and at the ending You… Eternal are remaining!
Your words spread out because of Your actions,
Your honour is because… You are neverending!
Praise be to You, great God the most excellent!
You stand alone, no match or equal is existing.
You count and You make happen… every hair:
the jewels on the thread of life You're stringing!
You are the critic of all the jewels of the Truth…
yet, all fine, all hidden things You're disclosing.
Yes, You're revealing whatever has been hidden
and whatever is obvious You're securely hiding.
You're the Architect of the House of Existence:
in vision's meadows it's You Who is satisfying.
O Lord, You help me, because I am so worried:
I'm bewildered, so miserable, humble I'm being.
I have no skill, except for a lack of skilfulness…
I've no knowledge of a gift to me You're giving!

Here I am, having fallen head-first into a role
that is strange: where is beginning and ending?
This occupation could be likened to a rocky hill
and a terrifying ocean, that my way is stopping.
Without Your help that You'd divinely shower,
and without Your kind grace that me is leading,
although I still wish to be gathering in the rocks
that ruby, and from seas that pearl be bringing;
without Your help, although my desire is there,
such desire without Your help is worth nothing!
So, bring enlightenment to enlighten my heart,
to my mind bring the light of… understanding,
so that the mirror of my heart may shine bright
and happily reach all the pages of my thinking
and be filling all of the fields of my prosperity…
the kindness of Your Prophet as rain be sending
so that I may discover the key to open the door,
so that I might discover the goal, of my longing!

*

KHAYALI (d. 1556). A highly endowed with poetic genius, was Muhammad Khayali Bey, who was called 'the lord and leader of the poets of this age'. Khayali was a native of Vardar Yenijesi, 'the meeting-place of poets and the well-spring of the accomplished.' When quite young he became a disciple of the mystic teacher Baba Ali-e-Mest, (Father Ali the Drunken), in whose service he gained an insight into spirituality to which his poems written later bear witness. His mind became indelibly impressed with the dervish ideal of a retired simple life, free from desire of worldly wealth and glory. Khayali wandered the country in company with his master and they finally came to Istanbul where they were brought to the notice of a judge of the city, who disapproved of the youthful disciple roaming with the wandering *kalandar,* and confined him to the care of a policeman at whose hands he received an education.

Khayali's poems which are for the most part deeply tinged with Sufism display far more originality both of thought and treatment than is usual with the poets of this age. *Qasidas* and *gazels* are in Khayali's *Divan* and other forms of poetry.

Translation from...

Wine, Blood & Roses: Anthology of Turkish Poets, Translations & introduction by Paul Smith, New Humanity Books, Campbells Creek, 2008.

I'm a Mejnun, filled with the grace of Leyla;

in my head's the passionate craze... of Leyla.

I am the plaything of fate and of evil fortune

who is drowning in ocean's maze... of Leyla.

To me, the bloody shrouded martyr of Love

is every tulip in those desert ways... of Leyla.

A Mejnun-like heart feels shame at honour,

when branded by the dear disgrace, of Leyla.

I am a silent Mejnun who is full of rapture...

but, in heart is the defining praise, of Leyla.

Falling on my ear is the tinkling of an anklet;

will there ever appear any trace... of Leyla?

Khayali, until you can see with the inner eye,

never will appear that loving face, of Leyla.

*

NEF'I (d. 1635). Nef'i was born near Erzurum and arrived in Istanbul (Constantinople) when he was thirty where he lived in obscurity, working in small government jobs. Later he was brought to the notice of Murat IV who became his patron. It was at his hands that the Turkish *qasida* attained its crowning point. The example of Urfi, the great Persian *qasida*-writer of the time influenced Nef'i's work. In this matter of the cultivation of the *qasida,* Nef'i's influence came to form a series of models for a host of subsequent writers, many of whom have done good work and earned for themselves a well-deserved reputation, but not one has been able to rival as a *qasida*-writer this gifted poet.

Nef'i also was excellent in writing mystical *ghazels* (see below) and satires that some people in high places found difficult to digest.

Translation from...

Wine, Blood & Roses: Anthology of Turkish Poets, Translations &
introduction by Paul Smith, New Humanity Books, Campbells
Creek, 2008.

With your long hair can't the lover chain up the mad heart that

like Mejnun's cannot be ruled... or what may the lover be

doing?

Nef'i's always longing to be showing such bitter pain to you,

have some pity and one day that wound in this heart be

seeking.

*

SARMAD (d. 1659). Sarmad or Hazrat Sarmad Shaheed,
whose name 'Samad' derives from the Persian word for eternal
or everlasting, was a Persian dervish poet of Jewish and
Armenian origin. He had an excellent command of both
Persian and Arabic, essential for his work as a merchant.
Hearing that precious items and works of art were being
purchased in India at high prices, Sarmad gathered together his
wares and traveled to India where he intended to sell them.
He arrived in India from a Jewish, Persian-speaking Armenian
merchant family, soon to renounce his religion and adopted
Islam which he allegedly later renounced in favor of Hinduism
which he is also supposed to have renounced for Sufism.

Sarmad was known for exposing and ridiculing the major
religions of his day, but also wrote beautiful religious poetry in
the form of *rubai's*. He wandered the streets and the courts of
the emperor completely naked (like Baba Tahir... perhaps a

major influence), and to have fallen in love with a 14 year old Hindu boy in a spiritual sense. He was close to Dara Shikoh, the heir presumptive to Emperor Shah Jahan. During his life he produced a translation of the *Torah* into Persian. Finally, he was beheaded in 1659 by the emperor Aurangzeb for his perceived heretical poetry. Sarmad's ambiguous religious affiliation is disputed today by Jews, Muslims and Hindus.

Translation from...

Ruba'iyat of Sarmad, Translation & Introduction by Paul Smith, New Humanity Books, Campbells Creek, 2010.

This heart for its Layla, into a Majnun

has turned...

into a wilderness my home has become,

has turned.

In old age a pious one, youth's passion

has turned...

and the vagary of spring, with autumn

has turned.

*

MAKHFI (1639-1702). Princess Zeb-un-Nissa... (pen-name 'Makhfi') was the oldest daughter of the Mogul Emperor Aurungzeb of India. She revealed great intelligence from an early age and so received teaching. She discovered she had a remarkable memory and by the age of seven she had like Hafiz become a *hafiz,* one who had learnt the whole of the *Koran* by heart. Her proud father gave an enormous feast to celebrate, all his army in Delhi were feasted and the poor were given gold, businesses were closed for days.

A woman called Miyabai was hired as her teacher and in four years she had learnt Arabic, then mathematics and astronomy. She started to write a commentary on the *Koran* but her father objected and she had to stop. She had written poems from a young age in Arabic but a scholar from Arabia commented, "These are wise and clever poems and it is a miracle that a foreigner knows Arabic so well, but… it is still obvious that they were composed by an Indian." Being a perfectionist, from then on she only composed her poems in Persian.

At first she wrote her poetry in secret but her tutor, a scholar named Shah Rustom Ghazi, found her poems and prophesised her future greatness and went to her father and persuaded him to search India and Persia to find poets and bring them to come to Delhi to become a circle of poets surrounding her. She never married and was eventually imprisoned by her father for many years for being involved in a plot with her brother to unseat him and for her Sufi beliefs. She eventually died in prison.

Translations from…

Makhfi: The Princess Sufi Poet Zeb-un-Nissa, A selection of Poems from her Divan, Translation & Introduction by Paul Smith, New Humanity Books, Campbells Creek, 2006.

Proud Beloved, at Your feet I lay brow's pride; I am as

near Your heart as Your coat, why "You're a stranger,"

express?

O Makhfi, like Majnun walk proudly in grief's valley

with new dedication gird yourself, love's promise... no

less!

If you are led by dangerous love and enter the Master's path,

in desert like Majnun you'll stay always, never to look back:

start

to know this, you'll not even care if you lose your life or not,

pain ignore, not to seek shore of love's limitless ocean you'll

depart.

Within the desert of a world gone astray how

many weary wanderers their way were losing!

Love, with beckoning hand, appears to bless,

through the wilderness a way them is finding;

and though like Majnun in the wild they roam

through toils and trials them, home is leading.

Burning heart, how long can you keep hidden, see... flames

flare

and smoke from your sighs even the stars in the sky make

disappear.

Driven by love I must wander like Majnun where desert's

dust falls on tired head, eternally for Layla to cry many a

tear.

Mine is pure love that pursues its quest through desert and

wilderness:

mine is the lonely cry... Majnun's heart, tears, torn clothes

weariness.

Mine is work taking all breath, pain's cry, strife's agony...

life lived longing for death, for more dear than life becomes

lifelessness.

*

ABDUL-KADIR (b. 1652). A son of the great Afghan poet Khushal Khan, Abdul-Kadir Khan is considered to be the most eloquent writer and poet of all Khushal's sons.

Like his father Abdul-Kadir was as good at the sword as at the pen; and in the battle with the Mughal troops at Kottah in the Peshawar district the victory of the Afghans was chiefly owing to the skill displayed by the poet.

The poems of Abdul-Kadir in Pushtu which are deeply imbued with Sufism are thought of very highly by the Afghans and his language is extremely polished. His chief works now known are a *Divan* from which the following *ghazals* are taken; a translation of Jami's *Yusuf and Zulikha* from the Dari, which is considered the most perfect of its kind in the Afghan language; also translations of Sadi's *Gulistan* and *Bostan*, from the Dari in Pushtu. He is said to have been the author of sixty different works.

Translation from…

Tongues on Fire: Anthology of Sufi, Dervish, Warrior & Court Poets of Afghanistan, Translation & Introduction by Paul Smith, New Humanity Books, Campbells Creek, 2008.

Those are red tears you see that are by unhappy Majnun shed,

for the tulip has neither in mountain nor in meadow been

blooming

Abdul-Kadir, it is time to set out on path of non-existence…

possibly there, you might a trace of the Beloved's door be

finding!

Criticised by the world, into the wilderness I'll flee;

just like Majnun I'll make my home the wilderness!

The fruit shall then eat from its aims and its desires,

when in earth grain gives itself to extinction, no less.

*

RAHMAN BABA (1652-1711). Abdul Rahman (respectfully referred to as Rahman Baba) is considered by many to be the greatest Sufi Pashtun poet to compose poems, mainly *ghazals,* in the Pushtu language.

Rahman Baba was born in the seventeenth century in the hilly Mohmand region of Afghanistan, outside of Peshawar. He was called 'The Nightingale of Peshawar'. This was a time when Afghanistan was under invasion by the Persians to the west and the Mongols to the east, a period of great struggle and hardship.

Yet, in the midst of this turmoil, the young Abdul Rahman showed himself to be an excellent student with a natural gift for poetry. But as he grew older he became disillusioned, questioning the real value of such pursuits. He withdrew from the world, becoming a hermit, dedicating himself to prayer and devotion. In his solitary worship... he began to write poetry, again.

Despite his reclusive life, Rahman Baba's poetry quickly spread and gained fame. Religious figures used his poetry to inspire the devout. Political leaders used his poems to inspire the independence movement. Rahman Baba's poetry became an important part of the nation's voice. In 2009 the Taliban blew up his tomb near Peshawar.

His *Divan* consists of 343 poems... *ghazals* and a few *qasidas and mukhammas*. Hafiz (many of Rahman's *ghazals* resemble his) and Sana'i were two major influences on him, but also the poems of Rumi, Iraqi and Jami.

Translation from...

Rahman Baba: Selected Poems. Translation & Introduction by Paul Smith, New Humanity Books, Campbells Creek, 2010.

Majnun, who laid his head at the feet of his beloved Layla,

was famous in Arabia and foreign lands for the lover's art.

Those powerful always triumph over those who are weak;

I'm shielded from other misery by grief for my Sweetheart.

Why then, is tranquility prohibited to all of those, who

have to the caravan of this world, gone... then entered?

As to the state of Majnun, why should anyone inquire?

This world's state is Majnun, Layla too... enough said.

Love has breathed upon this universe a spell, so potent,

the lover, though keen of sight, is blind to all else ahead.

*

BEDIL (1644-1721). Mirza Abdul-Qader Bedil is one of the most respected poets in Afghanistan. In the early 17th century, his family moved from Afghan Turkestan (Balkh region) to India, to live under the Moghul dynasty. Bedil himself, although ethnically an Uzbek, was born and educated in India, near Patna. In his later life he spent time travelling and visiting his ancestral lands. His writings in Persian are extensive. He was greatly influenced by Hafiz. His *Kulliyat* (complete works) consist of many *ghazals, rubai's, tarkib-bands,* a *tarjih-band, mu'ammas* (riddles) and more. He also wrote four *masnavis,* the most important being *Irfaan,* which he completed at age 68. It contains many stories and fairy tales, outlining his philosophical views. Bedil's 16 books of poetry contain nearly 147,000 couplets. With Ghalib he is considered a master of the complicated 'Indian Style' of *ghazal.*

Possibly as a result of being brought up in such a mixed religious environment, Bedil had considerably more tolerant views than his poetic contemporaries. He preferred free thought to accepting the established beliefs of his time, siding with the common people and rejecting the clergy who he often saw as corrupt. He essentially believed that the world was eternal, and in constant motion. He believed that all life was first mineral, then plant, then animal. He also expressed disbelief in judgement day and other orthodox tenets of faith. Despite this, he was by no means an atheist or a freethinker in the modern day sense. On the contrary, he had complicated views on the nature of God, heavily influenced by the Sufis (with whom he spent a considerable period of time).

Bedil enjoyed virtually no fame in Iran and only few scholars knew of him until recently. In Afghanistan and Tajikistan however, he had a following that almost followed like a cult. People would get together at weekly Bedil meetings to study and interpret his poetry, and he was the poet of choice for many *ghazal* singers.

Translation from...

Unity in Diversity: Anthology of Sufi and Dervish Poets of the Indian-Subcontinent, Translation & Introduction by Paul Smith, New Humanity Books, Campbells Creek, 2003.

This world with the mania of 'me' and 'we' is malicious;

where is a love, that lust is not contaminating... tell us?

All these stories you are hearing of Majnun and Farhad,

are no more than sounds and words of poets... not for us.

All over the world illumination, like lightning...

I saw,

no dust was following the litter, Layla beaming,

I saw.

From the collyrium that Truth had applied to my eyes,

wherever a word... up was rising, the meaning

I saw.

O my Lord, deep into love I was falling...

what heart does to me I wasn't knowing.

Even I am finding that my heart is crazy:

I saw that one and enchanted became me!

In this love I became like famous Majnun,

for this heart I discovered lying in a ruin!

*

HAMID (1666-1730). Abdul Hamid Mohmand was born in the small village of Masho, belonging to the Afghan tribe of Mohmand... one of the purely Afghan tribes dwelling in the Peshawar district. Hamid, like Rahman Baba (above), was a Mohmand, but of a different clan. He was brought up into the clergy and is said to have gained a considerable amount of learning at Peshawar and students from all parts of the surrounding districts sought out his instruction.

He is the 'cynical poet' of the Afghans, the Shaikh Sadi of the Pushtu language. The beauty of his compositions is fully acknowledged among a nation so rich in poets in Persian (Dari) and Pushtu. He was sometimes called... 'Hamid, the Hair-splitter'. His poetry, although generally of a moral character, breathing contempt for the world and all of its vanities... is still tinged with Sufism and he is obviously influenced by the greatest master of the *ghazal,* Hafiz.

Translation from...

Tongues on Fire: Anthology of Sufi, Dervish, Warrior & Court Poets of Afghanistan, Translation & Introduction by Paul Smith, New Humanity Books, Campbells Creek, 2008.

Whoever enters on the path of love has to endure its pains:

for this is an excellent present to send the bride, to acquire.

When I saw Hamid, over head and ears in love's affairs,

I found him truly mad... Majnun's older brother to admire!

*

KHWAJA MOHAMMAD (born mid-late 17th C.). Little is known about him except that he lived in the reign of the fundamentalist Mughal emperor Aurangzeb and belonged to the Bangash tribe of Afghans who ruled the valley of that name and of which Kohatt is the chief town. Khwaja Mohammad lived the life of a dervish and followed the tenets of the Chisthi sect. He was a disciple of Rahman Baba (above), who was a disciple of Mi'an Panju a celebrated Sufi Master who came originally from India and dwelt for many years in Afghanistan.

His *Divan* is a very rare book. His *ghazals* in Pushtu are deeply mystical but occasionally he devotes a poem to the remembrance of lost friend.

Translations from...

Tongues on Fire: Anthology of Sufi, Dervish, Warrior & Court Poets of Afghanistan, Translation & Introduction by Paul Smith, New Humanity Books, Campbells Creek, 2008.

And love has brought scandal both in this world and the

next...

on one named Majnun and on the son of Hallaj, named

Mansur.

And what would the hunter in the forest ever know about

it,

if the partridge didn't signal him by calling so loud and

clear?

If you have the love and the attention of the Almighty...

from brother and friend you'll tear yourself away quickly.

Like Majnun, you will begin to wander in the wilderness:

thorns and brambles by the way, you will never even see.

*

MIR (1723-20th September 1810). Mir Taqi Mir whose original name was Mohammed Taqi was the leading Urdu poet of the eighteenth century and one of the pioneers who gave shape to Urdu. He was one of the principal poets of the Delhi school of the Urdu *ghazal*.

Like many Urdu poets Mir's literary reputation is from his *ghazals*. He lived at a time when the Urdu language and poetry was still at a formative stage. Basing his language on his native Hindi, he kneaded it with a sprinkling of Persian diction and phrases and created a poetic language at once simple, natural and elegant, influencing future poets.

Like Obeyd Zakani and others before him Mir practiced the *Malamati* or 'Blameworthy' aspect of Sufism. Using this way one ascribes to oneself an unconventional aspect of a person or society then plays out its results either in action or in poetry. He was a prolific writer, his complete works or *Kulliyat* consisting of 6 *Divans,* containing 13,585 couplets comprising all kinds of poetic forms: *ghazals, masnavis, qit'as, qasidas, ruba'is,* etc.

Translation from…

Love's Agony & Bliss: Anthology of Urdu Poetry, Translation & Introduction by Paul Smith, New Humanity Books, Campbells Creek, 2007.

Majnun, chasing the caravan without a reason is

man?

The fact is, he's clever, though seemingly mad, this

man.

Let's not deny that the priest's an angel, but he needs

to do much for us to describe him… with emphasis:

"Man!"

*

NAZIR (1735-1846). Nazir Akbarabadi (real name Wali Muhammad) was an Indian poet who wrote in Urdu. It is said that Nazir's poetic output consisted of about 200,000 couplets but unfortunately a bigger portion of it is destroyed and only 6000 couplets still exist. No other Urdu poet used as many words as Nazir.

Nazir's genius was not recognised until much later. In spite of this neglect, some of his 600 *ghazals* and other forms including *tarji-bands* (see below) are still available. He was young during the age of Sauda and Mir.

He was influenced by Amir Khusraw, Sadi, Rumi and like many other Urdu poets especially Hafiz whom he often quotes. He eventually renounced all wealth for a life of poverty. His lack of interest in things of the world showed in that he never collected his own poetry. He was said to have been a great musician. It is also said that he became God-realized. His poems are loved by folk today.

Translation from...

Love's Agony & Bliss: Anthology of Urdu Poetry, Translation & Introduction by Paul Smith, New Humanity Books, Campbells Creek, 2007.

I was perplexed! Where now to go? Where does He dwell?

Who to ask, how to find Beloved and on Him be gazing?

It was like this I was thinking, as like Majnun I wandered,

and still not even a trace was I discovering of my Beloved.

*

GALIB (1757-1799). Muhmad Es'ad known as Seyh or Sheykh Galib is considered to be the last great Turkish poet of the classical Ottoman tradition. Born and educated in Istanbul he was the son of an official of the government who would also play the drum in the order of the Mevlevi dervishes (the order established by Rumi's son).

He tried like his father to combine a position in the civil-service of the government with his spiritual life as a dervish but eventually failed and went on to completely devote himself to the spiritual way and became the sheykh of the Galata lodge or convent of the Mevlevi order.

Apart from his *Divan* consisting mainly of spiritual *gazels*, he composed a famous, great masterpiece *mesnevi*, the allegorical and truly spiritual *Beauty and Love* composed when he was only 21, which is original in every way and considered one of the world's finest mystical poems. In prose he wrote two books on Sufism and a biographical work on Mevlevi poets.

Translation from…

Wine, Blood & Roses: Anthology of Turkish Poets, Translations & introduction by Paul Smith, New Humanity Books, Campbells Creek, 2008.

I'm that Mejnun over there, upon whose head their nests

are shaking, trembling and rearing,

in this mystic dance!

O Galib, while the Sun of Love is pouring out radiance,

Mevlevis will like motes be turning

in this mystic dance.

GHALIB (1797-1869). Mirza Asadullah Beg, known as Ghalib (conqueror), a pen-name or *takhallus* he adopted in the tradition of all classical Urdu poets, was born in the city of Agra of parents with Turkish aristocratic ancestry.

Ghalib's early education has always been a matter of confusion. Around 1810, he was married into a family of nobles, at the age of thirteen. He had seven children, none of whom survived (this pain has found its echo in some of his *ghazals*). He had himself remarked during his lifetime that although his age had ignored his greatness, it would be recognised by later generations. History has vindicated his claim.

Although Ghalib wrote in Persian as well, he is more famous for his *ghazals* written in Urdu (approx. 235 of them). It is believed he wrote most of his popular *ghazals* by the age of nineteen. His *ghazals*, unlike those of Mir, contain highly personalised Urdu and are therefore not easily understood or appreciated by a vast majority of people without extra effort. His *Divan* contains 263 *ghazals* and a small number of *ruba'is*, *masnavis*, *qasidas* and *qit'as*.

There have been many movies based on his life made in India and Pakistan where his popularity has never flagged.

Translation from...

Love's Agony & Bliss: Anthology of Urdu Poetry, Translation & Introduction by Paul Smith, New Humanity Books, Campbells Creek, 2007.

Majnun's burning sighs are light and eyes of desert;

if not Layla's lamp, all night shining too...

no matter!

To enliven a house there must be some kind of noise:

a joyful poem or a sad elegy that is true…

no matter.

Held back by faith, towards not believing I'm drawn:

I have turned from *Kaaba,* a temple alluring

to me is!

I am the type of lover, who is misleading the beloved:

Majnun is criticized by Layla, if, comparing

to me is!

*

TAHIRAH (1817-1853). Tahirah (meaning 'concealed'), also called Qurrat'ul-'ayn (meaning: 'freshness of the eye') was Zarrin Taj Fatima, and this extremely beautiful and intelligent woman led a short and stormy life. Born (like Obeyd Zakani) in Qazvin she became a devotee of the Bab, who from Shiraz had given his prophetic message that would later appear in the form of Baha-ul-lah, the founder of the Baha'is and the self-proclaimed Imam Mahdi (Messiah). She was not only a poet but also wrote prose, knew literature, religious laws and interpretations of the *Koran* and lectured… very unusual for a woman of that time and previous times in Iran.

She travelled to Kerbala and Baghdad spreading the message of the Bab. In Baghdad she was arrested by the governor and sent back to Iran. She became the first woman to appear unveiled before a crowd of women and men. She returned to Qazvin after the Bab was killed and was soon after imprisoned in Tehran. She was thirty-six when sentenced to death after the Shah, who had proposed to her, which she rejected was assassinated leading to a massacre of the Baha'is.

Further Reading…

Princesses, Sufis, Dervishes, Martyrs and Feminists: Eight Great Women Poets of the East. Translations, Introduction by Paul Smith, New Humanity Books, Campbells Creek, 2008.

All of the glances of those eyes that keep on wandering,

each one that had any insight became totally transfixed.

From such a Majnun-like heart as this what power pours

that so many tents in Layla's pavilion are… obliterated.

*

IQBAL (1873-1938). Muhammad Iqbal was born in Sialkot, in the Punjab. He graduated from Government College, Lahore, in 1899 with a master's degree in philosophy. He taught there until 1905, while he established his reputation as an Urdu poet. During this period his poetry expressed an ardent Indian nationalism, but a marked change came over his views between 1905 and 1908 when he was studying for his doctorate at Cambridge University visiting German universities and qualifying as a barrister.

He turned to Islam and Sufism for inspiration and rejected nationalism as a disease of the West. These ideas found expression in the long *masnavi* poem *Asrar-e-Khudi (The Secrets of the Self)* in 1915 inspired by the *Masnavi* of Rumi, and *Rumuz-e-Bekhudi (The Mysteries of Selflessness)* in 1918.

These were written in Persian, not Urdu, presumably to gain his ideas an audience in the Muslim world outside India. When his long poem *Asrar-e Khudi* (Secrets of the Self) was published Iqbal attacked Hafiz for Iqbal's belief that Hafiz preached ascetic inaction. He later explained that the couplets he wrote on Hafiz were only illustrating and criticising a literary principle and shortly afterwards he praised Hafiz as one of the world's greatest poets and excluded from the poems the lines criticising Hafiz.

Many of Iqbal's *ghazals* resemble those of Hafiz and it is through the rhymes and metres he inherited from Hafiz, Ghalib and others, that he expounded his philosophy of Action and the realization of the Self.

Translation from...

Love's Agony & Bliss: Anthology of Urdu Poetry, Translation & Introduction by Paul Smith, New Humanity Books, Campbells Creek, 2007.

That One I sought over the earth and in the air too,

I discovered lived in my heart's abode... there, too!

If *Kaaba's* threshold knew obeisance's rule, to meet

those kneeling brows it would rise up in prayer, too!

O Majnun, did you ever happen to look at yourself?

Like Layla, you are behind the screen up there, too!

Majnun left the world, so let him the wilderness

abandon too:

if he seeks divine vision, let him Layla, no less...

191

abandon too.

Go and be shattering the mirror of fear, no matter how far,

go quickly and be breaking all of the bottles in the bazaar!

Like the reed-flute, be bringing a message from the reeds...

give to Majnun a message from Layla, one that he needs!

Go and now be creating a whole new style for your song,

enrich the feast with your piercing strains, loud and long!

*

ASGHAR (1884-1936). Asghar Hussain Gondvi was born at Gonda in India. His father Taffazul Hussain was a clerk who couldn't afford to educate his son in a good school or college. He studied only up to the 8th grade but he attained through hard work mastery of Urdu, Persian, Arabic and English.

In his youth he led a life of sensuous abandon, but later influenced by Sayed Abdul Ghani Kazmi, a religious saint and mystic, he led a life of piety and self-control. He loved literature, religion and philosophy, more specially, the way of the Sufi s.

Like Jigar (to follow) whom he influenced, Asghar also sometimes sold eye-glasses to earn a living.

Asghar like many poets in this anthology is a specialist of the *ghazal*. The central theme of his poetry is love, not earthly and material, but mystical, transcendental. He expresses his feelings with great artistry, using the imagery of romantic poetry, so that he can be enjoyed at the secular and spiritual levels.

For him life is a quest, an eternal search for the fountain of love and beauty and truth and analysis cannot take us to the source of light and love.

Translation from...

Love's Agony & Bliss: Anthology of Urdu Poetry, Translation & Introduction by Paul Smith, New Humanity Books, Campbells Creek, 2007.

Since the world began, love finding its goal in beauty... is:

Majnun's soul's with Layla, if riding on the camel, she is.

A long search is... life, a name for ceaselessly searching:

the secret of life always a goal in the distance, staying is.

*

HUMA (1894-1969). Merwan S. Irani, known world-wide as Meher Baba, took Huma (Phoenix) as his *takhallus* or pen-name when he composed *ghazals* in a mixture of Persian, Urdu and Gujarati in his twenties as an enlightened lover of the *Qutub* or Perfect Master Upasni Maharaj, and also later on. He knew the *ghazals* of Hafiz by heart as did his father, the dervish Sheriar Irani, who had originally walked to Poona in India from Khooramshah in Iran. Merwan went on to reveal himself as *Qutub* and later also declared himself as the *Rasool* or Messiah (Avatar).

He was a great lover of Sufi and Dervish Poetry and in particular that of Kabir and Hafiz whom he often explained and quoted and occasionally translated into impeccable and ground-breaking English versions, and in the early 1930's he caused Hafiz's tomb to be repaired and rebuilt.

Meher Baba is famous for keeping silent for over 40 years. He 'dropped his physical form' in 1969, quoting particular Hafiz couplets as he departed from this world.

Translation from...

Huma: Selected Poems of Meher Baba, Translation by Paul Smith, New Humanity Books, Campbells Creek, 2006.

O Meher, in Your heart is a love, belonging

to Majnun:

he lives there, Your court he was coming

to... Majnun.

Majnun, with each breath called in the desert, "Layla,"

and in Your court Layla kept on listening

to... Majnun.

Without that one, Majnun is pining away until he dies:

all life is Layla, Layla is the heart: according

to Majnun.

But Majnun saw Your light's radiance and forgot Layla:

a shout, "O Lord," in heart Lord was coming

to Majnun.

More of a murderer than Layla is God... for Him he had

to burn to ashes, though love was belonging

to Majnun.

For the sake of love Majnun was fire and became ashes:

but Beloved so cruel, for years gave suffering

to, Majnun!

O love for the world, do not be the ruination of me:

forget about me and I will forget you... completely!

Layla's beauty every breath of Majnun disclosed...

O Layla, you should have ignored him, obviously.

O Beloved, I am filled with pain in Your prison...

but, still I keep enjoying it, so... do not set me free.

O Meher, our Beloved; life, heart of everyone and thing

You are...

Guide, follower You are, Path You are, our Homecoming

You are!

You are Winebringer, wineshop and You are wine and lover...

You are Majnun, Layla; camel, caravan and litter following

You are.

Why go seeking Beloved in the world, for in your heart He

is...

all stations of the Path are in you, in each one you are... be

His!

It was love that made Majnun tormented and restless, worried,

Layla was sharing his love as on the camel's seat she felt

bliss!

*

PAUL (b. 1945). Paul Smith was born to middle-class parents in Melbourne, Australia. He began composing poems in the ancient Persian form of the *ghazal* at the age of 6 on his way to school, it was only 12 years later that through the poetry of Hafiz he discovered what this form was.

Over the past 45 years he has composed free-form poems, and for the first time in English, apart from translations... *ruba'is, ghazals, masnavis, qasidas* etc.

These poems were composed at home or travelling in the East and the U.S.A., while giving readings of his poetry and his many translations: poems about love and separation, evolution and God and man and the environment and the past, present and future.

His Spiritual Master was since 1966, and still is... Meher Baba (see his section under the pen-name of 'Huma').

Many of his own poems were composed while translating the works of Hafiz over 30 years and Sadi, Nizami, Rumi, Kabir, Obeyd Zakani, Jahan Khutan and many others (as in this book and other translations).
From...

The Master, Muse and Poet: An Autobiography in Poetry by Paul Smith. New Humanity Books, Campbells Creek, 2012.

I drown in the Ocean once more for Your love;
Your love is the killer, kill me more I implore!
They asked Majnun's name he said "Layla;"
You walk through that door... I am no more.

This diving for the pearl of Unity, all this holding one's
breath together... this *hamdami*... this conspiracy is so
deep and long and mysterious and breathtakingly deeply
nostalgic and blissful... that to be one Soul that's aglow
in two forms consciously is an act of such divine madness
that even Majnun and his Layla would happily let it flow!

If Love is the end of the road that desire is taking,
when from lust one's turned,
it's all or it's nothing.
When Majnun was told that Layla was given to
another, to desert he turned:
it's all or it's nothing.

Layla and Majnun: A Feature Film by Paul Smith

'Layla & Majnun' is one of the most famous and influential love stories of all time. It is a true story that probably inspired Shakespeare to write 'Romeo and Juliet'.

Of the many poetic versions of this immortal tale the one that has stood the test of time and influenced most others is by the great 12th century Persian poet Nizami that is written in over 4000 rhyming couplets that has been translated into many languages and has been told throughout the Middle East and elsewhere in songs, plays, operas and movies. The author of this film-script has used his own translations from his book of this work to form the narrative (by Nizami) and the dialogue and songs of all the participants to make this unique and important work of art, thus bringing to the viewer not only the scope of the story for the eye, emotion and heart but also the beauty, simplicity and profundity of the poetry of the story for the mind, feeling and soul.

LAYLA AND MAJNUN are the children of the leaders of two large and powerful feuding tribes in 7th century Arabia who meet at school and fall helplessly and hopelessly in love...

a love that will lead to war between the tribes, immortal songs of love and longing, madness, separation, scandal and disgrace, forced marriage, wanderings in the wilderness, friendship and betrayal, death and destruction of whole families and eventually the union of the two lost, tragic souls in a dramatic and heart-wrenching finale that transcends this material world.

Whether this feature-film be made with actors or with actors then animated via computer (as has recently been successfully done), it is a movie that would gain an audience of all ages in all countries.

NOTE: Funding for this project should not be too difficult if one looked towards the Middle-East and India.

IMPORTANT: On reading the following it will become evident that within the immortal poetry of the Narrator (Nizami) are the scene and actor directions in wonderful and colorful detail and this is the reason why only the barest of directions and scene settings have been given.

The complete script of this film is available from New Humanity Books.

The following is the opening 15 minutes of the film.

EXTERIOR & INTERIOR. MANSION IN ARABIA - DAY

The sun rises to reveal an elderly, distinguished-looking man in a robe and turban (SYED OMRI) looking out with a sad expression standing on the balcony of a large palace-like mansion in a city lying in the midst of a large oasis on the edge of a plain, then desert and rocky mountains.

NIZAMI (NARRATOR) (VOICE OVER)
Once there lived among the Bedouin in old Arabia
a lord, a Syed... Omri, ruling over the Banu Amir.
His success and his prosperity made him a leader
of many Arabs and he was as wealthy as Korah.
He helped the poor... his purse was always open:
to all strangers he was a generous host and when
he began a new venture he succeeded... as if good
luck he had, like stone in fruit: this, he understood!
The great man's heart was eaten by a secret grief:
he had all he wanted... but no son had this chief.

His face looks as worried as his thoughts...

SYED OMRI (V.O.)

Where will lie happiness? Where is shade to nest?

He stays alive, who in his son is seen and blessed.

Syed Omri is in prayer. Walking around his mansion through the vast, empty rooms... pleading with Allah... talking to himself, arguing with the WOMEN in his harem, blaming them... then finally on his knees again... begging for Allah's intervention.

NIZAMI (V.O.)

In this way this nobleman worried and the older he

became the greater became his need for a progeny.

For many years his alms and prayers were in vain:

moon never rose, that seed's offshoot never came.

Still, he was never content to bow to his destiny...

one wish not given... but all else he could not see!

That is how most of us are: if a prayer remains not

fulfilled... do we think it is what should be our lot?

We think we know, yet the future is veiled from us:

our fate's thread ends beyond the visible and thus

what today we mistook for a lock, keeping us out,

may later be the key... that, which we had sought.

He desired the jewel he did not have, so he prayed

and he begged until finally God his wish fulfilled.
He was given a boy who looked like a rose's smile:
the rose, whose petals keep opening all the while
one sleeps... like the diamond that can transform
the darkness of the world into a light... newborn!

The baby (QAYS-'MAJNUN') is beautiful, his is father
overcome with joy... his mother proud and is now first WIFE.
Syed Omri runs through his mansion calling his servants. The
poor are given gold at his instructions. All are happy for him
and sing his praises, thanking and blessing him.

NIZAMI (V.O.CONT.)
Overcome, the happy father opened wide the door
of his great treasury. All would share in his store
of happiness... and this event was then celebrated
with many blessings to the happy parents shouted.

Now the baby is being put in the care of an older lady...
somewhat GYPSY looking.

NIZAMI (V.O.CONT.)
The child was given to a caring nurse, so under
her careful eye he'd grow strong... and even stronger.

Lines drawn on his face to protect... magic on his soul:
this remained secret: hiding it, she knew her special role!

Alone in the child's room she looks around then draws magical
symbols on his face. Syed Omri and his wife look down on
their baby as the moon shines through the window and lights
his perfect face.

NIZAMI (V.O CONT.)
The child looked like the moon after fourteen days
and so his parents gave him the name of... Qays.

The boy grows up from one year old... cute and happy...
playful and mischievous until he is seven, a handsome face...
hair beginning to grow faintly on his upper lip.

NIZAMI (V.O.CONT.)
A year passed... and his beauty grew to perfection:
as light cuts water, in his form was love's reflection.
And when he turned seven the violet-coloured hair
of a first beard began to show on his cheek: there!

As he walks (now a ten year-old) through the rooms the
servants watch him pass in awe of his grace and, beauty and

charisma and quietly talk to each other about him.

NIZAMI (V.O.CONT.)
And when he had finally passed his first ten years
some spoke of his beauty like a fairy tale, in tears!

EXTERIOR. BAZAAR IN THE CITY - DAY

As he rides on a small white pony alongside his proud father on
a large beautiful Arabian steed followed by many servants in
carriages carrying caskets from which coins are scattered few
stoop to pick them up as most are mesmerized by the boy's
extraordinary appearance.

NIZAMI (V.O. CONT.)
And whoever did happen to see him... even if only
from afar... called on God to bless him, eternally.

INT/EXT. VERANDAH OF DESERT SCHOOL -
DAY

MAJNUN (aged 12) sits with about a dozen other
CHILDREN being taught by a white-bearded old
TEACHER as a new pupil is introduced to the class... ten
year old LAYLA.

NIZAMI (V.O. CONT.)

Look now on where instruction pours on the mind

the light of knowledge... both simple and refined;

each leader of a tribe has his children there... each

is studying what the old, bearded sage can teach.

So it was here young Qays, his knowledge drew...

and he scattered pearls from his lips of ruby hue;

it was here, of a different tribe and a gentler way,

a lovely maid of tender years came one fatal day:

her intelligence in its early bloom was to be found,

and her quiet body was clothed simply, but sound.

When this Arabian moon her bright cheek revealed...

a thousand hearts were won... no pride or shield,

could stop her beauty: it was impossible to resist!

She was given to enthrall, to charm: one, the most!

All the children stare at her fascinated by her beauty... but one
is the most affected and can't keep his eyes off her... Majnun!

NIZAMI (V.O. CONT.)

Her long, flowing curling locks were black as night

and she was called... Layla, that heart's delight...

just one glance and the nerves became distraught,

just one glance, bewildered became each thought.

She flashes a look at him and he almost swoons away. Now he cannot keep still or concentrate on the teacher or his book… all he wants to do is gaze across at her face.

NIZAMI (V.O. CONT.)
And, when over young Qays, love's blushing rose
spread its rare sweetness, from him fled all repose:
a tumultuous passion danced upon his hot brow…
a 'majnun', 'mad' for her, he knew not why or how:
he gazed upon her perfect cheek and as he gazed,
love's flaming candle intensely inside him blazed.

Eventually she cannot keep her eyes off him so attractive is his form and his love for her.

NIZAMI (V.O. CONT.)
And soon the same pleasure fed each other's heart:
love had won them and they never dreamt to part.
And while the other students looked at their books
these two stared back and read each other's looks!

'A year later' (CAPTION), while others read, write, listen they only gaze at each other.

NIZAMI (V.O. CONT.)

While the others various places in books explored,

those two sat and stared... the adorer and adored!

Their only taste was for love and love's sweet ties,

writing songs and love poems to each other's eyes.

Qays (Majnun) silently mouths a poem across to her and she

replies with one of her own. Tears fill both of their young eyes

from the beauty of their poetry and from the love that is

bursting out from their hearts towards each other.

NIZAMI (V.O. CONT.)

Yes... love triumphant had come, engrossing both

the hearts and thoughts of the girl and the youth!

EXT. A QUIET GLADE - DAY

'Another year passes'... CAPTION. Now they hate being

separated by the distance they must sit in the school. They

play truant to be together in a quiet glade by a pool or meet

after school, hide there staring into each other's eyes or reciting

poetry or playing hide and seek.

NIZAMI (V.O. CONT.)

Then in quiet secret talking they passed the hours:
their love was like the season, like the fair flowers
freshly strewn upon the path now opening to their
sweet, melting words that are soft as Summer air.

*Yet they do not realize that the other children are sometimes
watching them, talking among themselves excitedly, pointing
to the young lovers oblivious of them, so enraptured are they of
each other's form and feeling. Something must happen!*

NIZAMI (V.O. CONT.)

Immersed in love… young, and yet it was so deep,
they hoped all suspicion would be lulled to sleep…
wishing the others saw what they no longer were,
though all could see their hearts… as one they were.

*Now the watching children run off and meet up with some of
the others and tell them what they have seen and they all laugh
and run off to tell the others.*

NIZAMI (V.O.CONT.)

But by a worldly prudence that was uncontrolled,
in their every glance… their true feelings they told:

because true love never thinks of knowing the skill
of veiling those passionate looks of lovers, at will.

He stares at Layla's dark and beautiful, unique face.

NIZAMI (V.O. CONT.)

And when those black ringlets of a thousand curls,
and those lips of ruby... with those teeth of pearls,
and those dark eyes flashing, so quick and bright,
like the lightning on the brow of the darkest night...
when such charms as these their power display,
and they then steal one's bewildered heart away,
can any man living, openly lying, so coldly seem
to be totally unmoved as if by only a mere dream?

Majnun is gazing at her beauty, drinking it in.

NIZAMI (V.O.CONT.)

Young Majnun saw her great beauty, saw her grace,
and he saw the soft expression on her perfect face
then, no moment's rest he had by day or by night
because Layla was permanently there, in his sight.

Suddenly their teacher, flanked by Layla's maidservant and Majnun's manservant and followed by all the squealing, laughing children of the school rush to the young lovers in the glade and tear them away from each other and drag them off in separate directions and as they go they silently look back into each others eyes, tears streaming down their cheeks.

NIZAMI (V.O.CONT.)

But, when the fateful separation eventually came,
more brightly glowed this ardent lover's flame...
and Layla, in her deepest sorrow was also caught,
weeping about what upon them fate had brought.

As she is dragged further off he silently mouths her name again and again and again.

EXT. STREETS AND LANES OF THE CITY - DAY AND NIGHT

Distraught, Majnun wanders the streets, alleys, whispering her name... sighing, weeping. PEOPLE stop and stare and talk quietly amongst themselves about the sight of the son of Syed Omri's strange behaviour. Night falls and he continues his wandering, sighing and sobbing.

NIZAMI (V.O.CONT.)

He, now wandered wildly through lane and street,

walking like one insane, as if her he was to meet.

And now... so mad with all of this excessive grief,

into the lonely desert he wandered for some relief.

EXT. THE DESERT - DAY AND NIGHT

Finally, as the sun rises, he reaches the edge of the desert then

dashes into it.

NIZAMI (V.O.CONT.)

Eventually... as the morning dawned he ran away,

upon his head and his feet no covering did he lay...

He wanders blindly through the heat of the day, perspiration

running down his face and at night lays under the cold moon,

freezing, whispering her name into the cold, vast silence.

Finally he gets up and rushes off with some purpose in mind.

EXT. MANSION OF LAYLA'S PARENTS - SUNRISE

The sun creeps over a garden of a mansion, another city.

Majnun runs in desperation along a path and to its imposing front door and throws himself down and kisses the bottom of it.

NIZAMI (V.O.CONT.)

And then along the secret path he frantically goes

to where that mansion of Layla's parents arose...

then he kissed the mansion's door and in that kiss

he imagined he'd quaffed the cup of a divine bliss.

His face is bathed in bliss.

NIZAMI (V.O.CONT.)

How fast his feet moved to his sweetheart's place,

as if thousands of wings had quickened his pace...

but after he had his loving devotions to her paid...

many thousands of thorns, his way back him delayed.

This young lover who from his beloved was parted

now wandered, so depressed and broken-hearted.

He slowly picks himself up then turns and trudges back into

the desert, his clothes now rags from wandering in the desert

through thorny bushes... his hair dishevelled, his feet bare and

bloody. He finally wends his way to his hometown and

searches out some of his old friends.

NIZAMI (V.O.CONT.)

This unfortunate youth so absorbed in love's grief,

hoped that with his friends he'd find some relief:

a few of them, by a strong affection to him bound,

in midst of his troubles still faithful he now found.

But soon they become upset or bored by his distraction for

Layla and he can see this and realizing it isn't working heads

off into the desert again calling out her name again, again.

NIZAMI (V.O.CONT.)

Eventually... a useless refuge, friendship's smile...

his lovesick heart was beguiled for a short while...

and once again he rushed out into the wilderness,

for all he loved in life had vanished and in distress

he called out her magical name... but she was not

to be seen anywhere, and none of her family... not

anyone could he see in that wild, that lonely land:

he called her many times for he did not understand.

Exhausted... he falls down in the searing heat, sobbing...

whispering her name over and over but there is only one

answer... the great silence of this vast desert.

EXT. NAJD MOUNTAIN RETREAT - DAY

Layla walks restlessly, sobbing, around wild garden watched by her worried parents nearby.

NIZAMI (V.O.CONT.)

For Layla with all her family had been taken away
to far off Najd mountains... where they'd all stay.
Where she could think of only that one she loved...
and so her love grew deeper, as she slowly moved
restlessly around that wild mountainous retreat.

EXT. VARIOUS COUNTRYSIDE - DAY, NIGHT & EARLY MORN.

NIZAMI (V.O.CONT.)

Her poor lover Majnun went looking for her: to meet
her he looked in the rosy bower, each silent glade
where the tall palm-trees gave a refreshing shade.
He desperately called aloud her name once again...
again he called his beloved, again... again in vain:
her voice was not heard anywhere, on every side...
it was always his echo that to him sadly replied...

Layla, Layla, Layla! Her name rang out all around
as if all there were fascinated by its magic sound.
While an agonizing pain was stabbing in his chest
to the morning-breeze this song he addressed...

Majnun drops to his knees and begins singing to the early
morning breeze in his sweet voice... as soft flute music begins
in the background...

MAJNUN (SINGING)
O breeze of the morning, so fresh and so sweet...
will you go to my beautiful beloved to kindly greet
and, then nestling in her glossy, long flowing hair,
my tenderest thoughts... my love for her declare?

He now looks down and he whispers more of his song...

MAJNUN (CONT. SINGING)
Will you, while you are in her black curls playing,
their intoxicating scent... their perfume smelling,
tell to that loved one, my fair soul-seducing maid,
how from grief of separation down low I am laid!

He stops and looks around again to make sure that none are
near that may overhear him. Seeing no one he looks up again
into the breeze rustling the palm trees and sings out...

MAJNUN (CONT. SINGING)

And please... so gently whisper in her precious ear
this message that I give you, to her make it clear...

Majnun remembers Layla in the schoolyard gazing towards
him and at their secret places playing with him, laughing,
teasing him... so beautiful and loving in his eyes... sometimes
she dances for him.

MAJNUN (CONT. SINGING)

Your lovely form is staying always in my sight...
in thoughts through the day and dreams by night,
for this poor one, who is in spirits sad and broken,
your cheek's dark mole would be the happy token:
that black mole that always adds to each glance
a magical spell for which I can't take the chance...
for, that one who sees all of your melting charms
and does not feel his soul clasped inside his arms
bursting with such passion, with such rapture, all
that speaks of love's deepest and wildest thrall...

would be like mountain's summit, like ice... cold,

and probably not born out from the human mould.

Let the one who is not moved by charms like yours

give up his life, for no real life through him pours!

Those lips of yours are sugar, so heavenly sweet...

let only these lips... your sweet pouting lips meet!

As her lips come closer to give his a kiss ... We return to the
present with Majnun singing passionately to the morning
breeze rustling the palm trees...

MAJNUN (CONT. SINGING)

Balsam for this heart's pure delight your lips shed

and their radiant colour is like the ruby: ruby-red.

He turns from trees and now quietly sings to himself...

MAJNUN (CONT. SINGING)

The evil eye has now struck out at my poor heart,

but it was your beauty that hurried the fatal dart:

and there have been many flowers, of richest hue,

that did fall and then perished where they grew...

but your great beauty is like the sun in brightness,

your form's an angel of Paradise in pure lightness:

you are an incalculable treasure... which poets say
even all of the heavens would gladly steal away...
'Too good, and too pure, upon this earth to stay!'

Now the sunlight has totally eclipsed the soft, silvery
moonlight for the sun has completely risen and the golden light
strikes his young face like a slap and he shakes his head as if
coming out of a dream and stand up straight as if bathing in
that lights shower and he stretches up his skinny arms towards
the sky slowly turning from pink to orange and yawns and
breathes out her name as if it was his last breath on earth and
he shakes off the sand from the rags that barely cover him and
he purposefully strides off into the rising sun...

NIZAMI (V.O.)

As the morning broke, the sun with a golden light
eclipsed those twinkling stars, all silvery white...
Majnun, quickly rising, he now eagerly pursued
a pathway that wound towards Layla's solitude,
his heart full of longing... and, as he went along,
his lips breathed softly some passionate song...
some favorite poem... which tenderly expressed
feeling that was always inside his anxious breast.
He saw her as fresh as the morning's scented air:

Layla is walking in a garden

NIZAMI (V.O. CONT.)

he... himself, was exhausted by his constant care:

Majnun is wandering, crazily through city streets

NIZAMI (V.O. CONT.)

he saw her blooming just like the blushing rose...

He is imagining her bending over a rose, smelling its fragrance.

NIZAMI (V.O. CONT.)

he himself... was dejected by his numerous woes;

Majnun sits in the desert, his head buried in his hands,
weeping.

NIZAMI (V.O. CONT.)

he saw her like a kind of angel, so light and pure...

He imagines Layla coming towards him bathed in an ethereal
light.

NIZAMI (V.O. CONT.)

himself, he kept burning away like an iron on fire;

Majnun is screaming at the sun her name.

NIZAMI (V.O. CONT.)

her long black curls flowing loosely to the ground:

Layla is in her room undoing her hair that falls to the floor as she looks in a mirror.

NIZAMI (V.O. CONT.)

his tangled and matted hair by his love was bound.

Majnun is in the desert throwing dust onto his head of tangled hair.

APPENDIX FOUR

The Muslim World's First Opera: Layla & Majnun

Layla and Majnun was the first opera in Azerbaijan, the Caucasus and the East... performed for the first time in 1908. It was written by Uzeyir Hajibeyov.

The first performance was on January 12th in Baku at Taqyev theatre. It has been called the first Muslim world's opera. In the first performance Hussein Rabynsky was the lead as Majnun (see below) and Hajibeyov himself played violin.

Hajibeyov and his brother Jayhan re-wrote the poems for the opera based on the long poem by Azerbaijani poet Fuzuli (see a selection from Fuzuli in Appendix Two).

Most of his poems/songs remain unchanged. The opera became a founder of the unique new genre in the world's musical culture, which synthesizes Oriental and European musical forms.

This opera has been performed more than 20,000 times in Azerbaijan as well as in other countries such as Russia, Ukraine, Iran, Turkey, Georgia, Uzbekistan, Turkmenistan.

(Hussein Rabynsky as Majnun)

WORKS PUBLISHED OR SOON TO BE PUBLISHED BY NEW HUMANITY BOOKS

MOST 6" X 9" PAPERBACKS PERFECTBOUND

Many of the following titlse are already in KINDLE

TRANSLATIONS

(NOTE: All translations by Paul Smith are in clear, modern English and in the correct rhyme-structure of the originals and as close to the true meaning as possible.)

DIVAN OF HAFIZ
Revised Translation & Introduction by Paul Smith
This is a completely revised one volume edition of the only modern, poetic version of Hafiz's masterpiece of 791 *ghazals, masnavis, rubais* and other poems/songs. The spiritual and historical and human content is here in understandable, beautiful poetry: the correct rhyme-structure has been achieved, without intruding, in readable (and singable) English .
In the Introduction of 70 pages his life story is told in greater detail than any where else; his spirituality is explored, his influence on the life, poetry and art of the East and the West, the form and function of his poetry, and the use of his book as a worldly guide and spiritual oracle. His Book, like the *I Ching*, is one of the world's Great Oracles. Included are notes to most poems, glossary and selected bibliography and two indexes. First published in a two-volume hardback limited edition in 1986 the book quickly went out of print. 542 pages.

PERSIAN AND HAFIZ SCHOLARS AND ACADEMICS WHO HAVE COMMENTED ON PAUL SMITH'S FIRST VERSION OF HAFIZ'S *'DIVAN'.*
"It is not a joke... the English version of ALL the *ghazals* of Hafiz is a great feat and of paramount importance. I am astonished. If he comes to Iran I will kiss the fingertips that wrote such a masterpiece inspired by the Creator of all and I will lay down my head at his feet out of respect."
Dr. Mir Mohammad Taghavi (Dr. of Literature) Tehran.
"I have never seen such a good translation and I would like to write a book in Farsi and introduce his Introduction to Iranians." Mr B. Khorramshai, Academy of Philosophy, Tehran.
"Superb translations. 99% Hafiz 1% Paul Smith."Ali Akbar Shapurzman, translator of many mystical works in English to Persian and knower of

Hafiz's *Divan* off by heart.

"I was very impressed with the beauty of these books." Dr. R.K. Barz. Faculty of Asian Studies, Australian National University.

"Smith has probably put together the greatest collection of literary facts and history concerning Hafiz." Daniel Ladinsky (Penguin Books author of poems inspired by Hafiz).

HAFIZ – THE ORACLE
(For Lovers, Seekers, Pilgrims, and the God-Intoxicated).
Translation, Introduction & Interpretations by Paul Smith.
Hafiz's Divan has been used as an Oracle successfully by millions of people from all walks of life for the past 600 years. The practice of interpreting his poems has been going on in Iran for many centuries. Here are almost four hundred of his *ghazals* with insightful and clear interpretations by Paul Smith plus an Introduction that includes his life, poetry, spirituality and the history of the use of his book as one of the world's great Oracles. The correct rhyme-structure has been kept as well as the beauty and meaning of these beautiful, mystical poems. 441 pages

HAFIZ OF SHIRAZ.
The Life, Poetry and Times of the Immortal Persian Poet.
Three Volumes
by Paul Smith
Told through the eyes of Hafiz's lifelong friend and student Muhammad Gulandam, this long, historical novel/biography based on ten years of research and writing covers Hafiz's life from the age of eight in 1328 when his father dies and he goes to live with his Uncle Sadi, until after his death in 1392. Shiraz is under siege by the tyrant Mubariz and Hafiz's friend the king, Abu Ishak, is on the brink of madness and despair. Along the way Hafiz falls in love with his muse the beautiful Nabat, meets his Spiritual Master, marries and has a son. He teaches at University and befriends the liberated princess Jahan Khatun (Iran's greatest female poet) after being a student of the outrageous poet/jester Obeyd Zakani. He experiences kingdoms rise and fall, the people of his beloved city throwing out dictators, and the wrath of the false Sufi and black magician Shaikh Ali Kolah. This is a majestic love story on a level of great love, beauty and consciousness, full of action and adventure, immortal poetry and song, bravery and betrayal and destiny. After the bloodthirsty tyrant Mubariz takes control in Shiraz closing the winehouses, imprisoning Hafiz's friend the poet, Princess Jahan and forcing Obeyd Zakani to flee for his life. Abu Ishak is executed and the false Sufi Ali Kolah is now in control of religious morals. Eventually

Mubariz's son Shah Shuja takes control but tragedy strikes Hafiz and Jahan, and Nabat must suffer separation. Kingdoms rise and fall through treachery and wars but through it all the songs/*ghazals* of Hafiz and his minstrel friends help the brave Shirazis to carry on until finally Hafiz gives his Master Attar an ultimatum after 40 years of devotion... God-Realisation or else! Over 1900 pages. 3 vols.

PIERCING PEARLS: THE COMPLETE ANTHOLOGY OF
PERSIAN POETRY (Court, Sufi, Dervish, Satirical, Ribald, Prison &
Social Poetry from the 9th to the 20th century.) Volume One
Translations, Introduction and Notes by Paul Smith
This 2 volume anthology is the largest anthology of Persian Poetry ever published. The introduction contains a history and explanation of all the forms used by the poets, a short history of the Persian language, Sufism in Persian Poetry & a Glossary of Sufi & Dervish Symbols plus a Selected Bibliography.
With each selection of a particular poet is a brief biography plus a list of further reading. The correct rhyme-structure has been kept as well as the beauty and meaning of these beautiful, often mystical poems.
THE POETS... Volume One 9th to the 13th Century.
Abbas of Merv page 29, Hanzalah 30, Firuz 31, Abu Salik 32, Abu Shakur 33, Junaidi, 35, Shahid, 36, Rudaki 38, Agachi 48, Rabi'a Balkhi 49, Khusravani 57, Manjik 58, Daqiqi 60, Mantiki 67, Umarah 69, Kisa'i 70, Firdausi 74, Baba Tahir 83, Farrukhi 88, Asjadi 100, Manuchirhri 101, Gurgani 106, Unsuri 110, Abu Said 116, Ibn Sina 123, Baba Kuhi 125, Nasir-i-Khusraw 127, Asadi 131, Azraqi 137, Qatran 140, Ansari 145, Al-Ghazali 147, Mas'ud Sad 149, Mu'izzi 159, Hamadani 168, Omar Khayyam 172, Sana'i 174, Sabir 189, Mahsati 182, Jabali 193, Vatvat 197, Anvari 201, Falaki 212, Khaqani 229, Zahir 242, Nizami 252, Ruzbihan 286, Baghdadi 288, 'Attar 290, Auhad ud-din Kermani 315, Kamal ad-din 320, Hamavi 325, Baba Afzal 328, Rumi 331, Imami 389, Hamgar 390, Sadi 395, Iraki 439, Humam 452, Amir Khusraw 457, Hasan Dilhavi 473, Simnani 475, Auhadi 478, Ibn Yamin 484, Khaju 490. Pages... 532

PIERCING PEARLS: THE COMPLETE ANTHOLOGY OF
PERSIAN POETRY (Court, Sufi, Dervish, Satirical, Ribald, Prison &
Social Poetry from the 9th to the 20th century.) Vol. Two Translations,
Introduction and Notes by Paul Smith
This 2 volume anthology is the largest anthology of Persian Poetry ever published. The introduction contains a history and explanation of all the forms used by the poets, a short history of the Persian language, Sufism in

Persian Poetry & a Glossary of Sufi & Dervish Symbols plus a Selected Bibliography. Included with each selection of a particular poet is a brief biography plus a list of further reading. The rhyme-structure has been kept as well as the beauty and meaning of these beautiful, often mystical poems. THE POETS: Volume Two... 14th Century to Modern Times ...Obeyd Zakani page 27, Emad 63, Salman 76, Shahin 84, Hafiz 105, Ruh Attar 173, Haydar 189, Azad 203, Junaid Shirazi 206, Jahan Khatun 211, Shah Shuja 244, Kamal 249, Maghribi 253, Bushaq 263, Kasim Anwar 276, Shah Ni'tmu'llah 284, Jami 291, Fighani 309, Babur 314, Humayan 317, Kamran 319, Ghazali 321, Kahi 323, Akbar 325, Urfi 326, Hayati 331, Ulfati 332, Dara Shikoh 333, Sarmad 336, Sa'ib 343, Nasir Ali 347, Makhfi 348, Bedil 358, Mushtaq 366, Hatif 370, Tahirah 377, Iqbal 392, Parvin 398, Khalili 423, Rahi 426, Simin 428. Pages 490.

DIVAN OF SADI: His Mystical Love-Poetry.
Translation & Introduction by Paul Smith
Sadi's mystical love poetry, his *ghazals*, although almost unknown in the West, are loved by his fellow-countrymen almost as much as those of Hafiz whom he greatly influenced. Here for the first time in English they can be read in all their beauty and power and spirit. The correct rhyme-structure has been kept as well as the beauty and meaning of these beautiful, mystical poems. ALL of the wonderful 603 *ghazals* from Sadi's *Badayi* and *Tayyibat* have been translated in clear, modern, meaningful, correct-rhyming English. Included is an Introduction containing The Life of Sadi, his Poetry and his influence on the East and the West and on the form and meaning of the *ghazal*. 421 pages.

RUBA'IYAT OF SADI
Translation & Introduction by Paul Smith
Here for the first time in beautiful English are eighty-eight of Sadi's wonderful short poems or *ruba'is* in the correct rhyme-structure and with all the meanings. Some are mystical others romantic, satirical and humourous and others critical of the selfishness of the time, of all time. As fresh today as they were when they were composed some 800 years ago. Included is an Introduction containing The Life of Sadi, his Poetry and his influence on the East and the West and a history of the form of the *ruba'i* and examples by its greatest exponents. The correct rhyme-structure has been kept as well as the beauty and meaning of these beautiful, mystical poems. 133 pages.

WINE, BLOOD & ROSES: ANTHOLOGY OF TURKISH POETS
Sufi, Dervish, Divan, Court & Folk Poetry from the 14th – 20th Century
Translations, Introductions, Notes etc., by Paul Smith
Introduction includes chapters on…The Turkish Language, Turkish Poetry,
The *Ghazal* in Turkish Poetry, The *Roba'i* in Turkish Poetry, The *Mesnevi*
in Turkish Poetry, The *Qasida* in Turkish Poetry and a Glossary. Included
with each selection of a particular poet is a brief biography plus a list of
further reading. The correct rhyme-structure has been kept as well as the
beauty and meaning of these beautiful, often mystical poems.
THE POETS…Sultan Valad page 27, Yunus Emre 36, Kadi Burhan-ud-din
60, Nesimi 70, Ahmedi 87, Sheykhi 93, Ahmed Pasha 96, Mihri 100, Zeyneb
108, Jem 110, Necati 115, Zati 128, Pir Sultan 133, Khayali 140, Fuzuli 150,
Baqi 172, Huda'i 188, Nef'i 190, Yahya 200, Haleti 208, Na'ili 216, Niyazi
221, Nabi 229, Nedim 235, Fitnet 243, Galib 250, Esrar Dede 261, Leyla
Khanim 265, Veysel 268. Pages 273.

OBEYD ZAKANI: THE DERVISH JOKER.
A Selection of his Poetry, Prose, Satire, Jokes and Ribaldry.
Translation and Introduction by Paul Smith
Obeyd Zakani is an important a figure in Persian and Sufi literature and
poetry. His satire, humorous stories, ribald and obscene poems, social
commentary, mystical *ghazals*, prose, *ruba'is* and his famous epic *qasida*
'Mouse & Cat' are popular today and are more relevant than ever. He is
considered to be one of the world's greatest satirist and social-commentator
whose life and mystical poems had a great influence on his student and
friend Hafiz and many others. This is the largest selection of his work in
English. The correct rhyme-structure has been kept as well as the beauty
and meaning of these beautiful, sometimes mystical poems. 224 pages.

OBEYD ZAKANI'S > MOUSE & CAT ^ ^
(The Ultimate Edition)
Translation & Introduction etc by Paul Smith
Obeyd Zakani's *Mouse & Cat* is a satirical, epic fable in the poetic form of
the *qasida* that was influential at the time it was composed (14th C.) and has
remained so for the past 600 years. It is more than just a story for children
(that some say brought about the cartoon of Tom & Jerry)… it is a story of
the stupidity of the false power of those in power and a warning to all that
such blind ambition always leads to destruction at the hands of one even
more powerful. Here is a beautiful, poetic translation keeping to the correct
form of the famous *qasida* illustrated with unique Persian miniatures.

Included is a long Introduction on The Life, Times and Writings of Obeyd Zakani. Appendixes include... Examples of all other translations into English; Obeyd performs *Mouse & Cat* for a young prince (from the Novel/Biog. *Hafiz of Shiraz*); a 1940's Illustrated Persian edition of *Mouse & Cat*, The Corrected Persian Text of *Mouse & Cat* and The First Complete Translation into literal English in 1906. 169 pages.

THE GHAZAL: A WORLD ANTHOLOGY
Translations, Introductions, Notes, Etc. by Paul Smith
Introduction includes...The *Ghazal* in Arabic, Persian, Turkish, Urdu, Punjabi, Pushtu, Sindhi, Kashmiri & English Poetry. Glossary. Included with each selection of a particular poet is a brief biography plus a list of further reading. The correct rhyme-structure has been kept as well as the beauty and meaning of these beautiful, often mystical poems.
THE POETS...Hazrat Ali page 27, Rabi'a of Basra 28, Dhu'l-Nun 32, Mansur al-Hallaj 34, Khusravani 37, Shahid 38, Manjik 39, Rudaki 40, Rabi'a Balkhi 43, Daqiqi 47, Kisa'i 49, Firdausi 51, Unsuri 53, Baba Kuhi 56, Qatran 57, Mas'ud Sa'd 59, Mu'izzi 62, Sana'i 64, Sabir 67, Falaki 69, Jabali 72, Vatvat 74, Anvari 75, Khaqani 77, Nizami 80, 'Attar 84, Kamal ud-din 96, Ibn al-Farid 98, Ibn 'Arabi 101, Rumi 106, Imami 121, Sadi 122, Hamgar 154, Iraki 156, Humam 163, Yunus Emre 165, Amir Khusraw 177, Hasan Dilhavi 188, Auhadi 190, Ibn Yamin 192, Khaju 193, Obeyd Zakani 199, Emad 208, Salman 218, Azad 221, Hafiz 224, Ruh Attar 264, Haydar 269, Junaid Shirazi 274, Kadi Burhan-ud-din 278, Jahan Khatun 281, Kamal 302, Maghribi 305, Nesimi 314, Bushaq 325, Shah Ni'matu'llah 337, Ahmedi 339, Sheykhi 343, Kasim Anwar 345, Jami 350, Baba Fighani 363, Babur 368, Ahmed Pasha 370, Mihri 372, Zeyneb 377, Jem 379, Necati 382, Zati 386, Pir Sultan 390, Khayali 394, Kamran 401, Fuzuli 402, Huda'i 412, Kahi 414, Baqi 416, Urfi 422, Yahya 425, Qutub Shah 428, Mirza 431, Haleti 442, Sa'ib 444. Na'ili 446, Niyazi 449. Khushal 452, Ashraf Khan 467, Makhfi 473, Nabi 507, Bedil 510, Abdul-Khadir 514, Rahman Baba 521, Khwaja Mohammad 536, Hamid 547, Wali 557, Nedim 561, Mushtaq 565, Ali Haider 567, Fitnet 568, Sauda 573, Dard 575, Ahmad Shah 578, Shaida 486, Nazir 592, Mir 599, Sachal Sarmast 606, Galib 611, Esrar Dede 618, Lelya Khanim 620, Mahmud Gami 621, Aatish 623, Zauq 627, Ghalib 630, Momin 636, Tahirah 639, Shad 647, Iqbal 651, Ashgar 657, Mahjoor 660, Jigar 613, Huma 669, Veysel 695, Firaq 699, Josh 704, Parvin 707, Rahi 713, Faiz 715, Simin 717, Paul 719. Pages 758.

NIZAMI: THE TREASURY OF MYSTERIES
Translation & Introduction by Paul Smith
"The Makhzanol Asrar (The Treasury of Mysteries), the most beautiful mystic poem in the Persian language, has both perfection of language and grandeur of thought. Every line of his Treasury of Mysteries is a living witness to his absolute certainty that piety, devotion, humility and self-forgetfulness are the corner stones of total annihilation, which in turn is necessary for unification with God and the foundation of the edifice of eternal life." G. H. Darab. Senior lecturer in Persian. University of London. Paul Smith has kept to the correct rhyme-structure while retaining the meaning and beauty of the original in simple, understandable, poetic English. He has written a long Introduction on the Life of Nizami and chapters on each of his books of poetry. Bibliography. 245 pages.

NIZAMI: LAYLA AND MAJNUN
Translation & Introduction by Paul Smith
It is impossible to underestimate the effect of Nizami's 'Layla and Majnun' on the world over the past 800 years. Many poets throughout this period have copied or been influenced by his story of the young lovers. Many Master-Poets besides Ibn Arabi, Attar, Rumi, Sadi, Hafiz and Jami have quoted from him or like him have used the story of the desperate lovers to illustrate how human love can be transformed into divine love through separation and longing. It is said that no one has painted a more perfect picture of women in Persian Literature than Nizami.
Paul Smith has kept to the correct rhyme-structure of this long *masnavi* epic poem, while retaining the beauty of the poetry, the mystical meaning and simplicity of the form. He has included a long Introduction on his life and chapters on all of the works of this great Master/Poet. Selected Bibliography. 216 pages.

UNITY IN DIVERSITY: Anthology of Sufi and Dervish Poets of the Indian Sub-Continent
Translations, Introductions, Notes, Etc. by Paul Smith
Introduction includes...Sufis & Dervishes: Their Art and Use of Poetry; Glossary of Sufi and Dervish Symbols; The Main Forms in Persian, Hindi, Urdu, Punjabi, Sindhi & Kashmiri Sufi & Dervish Poetry of the Indian Sub-Continent. Included with each selection of a particular poet is a brief biography plus a list of further reading. The correct rhyme-structure has been kept as well as the beauty and meaning of these beautiful, mystical poems. THE POETS... Baba Farid page 37, Amir Khusraw 45, Hasan

Dihlavi 57, Lalla Ded 59, Kabir 62, Qutub Shah 77, Dara Shikoh 80, Sarmad 83, Sultan Bahu 93, Nasir Ali 98, Makhfi 100, Wali 138, Bulleh Shah 143, Shah Latif 151, Ali Haider 160, Sauda 164, Dard 168, Nazir 173, Mir 189, Sachal Sarmast 204, Aatish 211, Zauq 217, Dabir 221, Anees 223, Hali 225, Farid 227, Shad 230, Iqbal 236, Inayat Khan 249, Asghar 266, Jigar 269, Huma 275, Firaq 307, Josh 312. Pages... 325.

RUBA'IYAT OF RUMI
Translation, Introduction and Notes by Paul Smith
Here are 330 wonderful *ruba'is* of the great Spiritual Master of the 13th century, who has become today the most popular poet in the world, Jelal ad-din Rumi: they are powerful, spiritual and full of joy, bliss and understanding. Unlike those of Omar Khayyam's these are poems composed by a soul before and *after* gaining God-realisation. Included in the Introduction is the life of Rumi and a history of the *ruba'i* and examples by its greatest exponents. Selected Bibliography. The correct rhyme-structure has been kept as well as the beauty and meaning of these immortal four-line poems. 368 pages.

RUMI: SELECTED POEMS
Translation, Introduction & Notes by Paul Smith
Included in the Introduction is the life of Rumi and chapters on the *ruba'i*, the *ghazal*, the *masnavi and the qasida*. Selected Bibliography. Glossary. The correct rhyme-structure has been kept as well as the beauty and meaning of these immortal poems of this most popular Perfect Spiritual Master and Master Poet. 217 pages.

THE MASNAVI: A WORLD ANTHOLOGY
Translations, Introduction and Notes by Paul Smith
Introduction includes... Article on the *masnavi* in various languages. With each selection of a particular poet is a brief biography plus a list of further reading. The correct rhyme-structure has been kept as well as the beauty and meaning of these beautiful, often mystical poems.
THE POETS...Abu Shakur page 13, Rabi'a Balkhi 15, Daqiqi 21, Firdausi 26, Gurgani 35, Nasir-i-Khusraw 39, Asadi 43, Sana'i 44, Khaqani 49, Zahir 52, Nizami 55, 'Attar 83, Rumi 91, Sadi 128, Sultan Valad 135, Yunus Emre 140, Amir Khusraw 144, Auhadi 149, Khaju 152, Obeyd Zakani 152, Shahin 157, Hafiz 178, Ruh Attar 192, Kasim Anwar 196, Shah Ni'tmu'llah 200, Jami 207, Fuzuli 207, Mir 210, Tahirah 219, Iqbal 225, Inayat Khan 231, Parvin 248, Paul 257. 268 pages.

HAFIZ'S FRIEND, JAHAN KHATUN: The Persian Princess Dervish
Poet... A Selection of Poems from her *Divan*
Translated by Paul Smith and Rezvaneh Pashai.
Daughter of the king of one of Shiraz's most turbulent times (8th century
A.H. 14th century A.D.) ... Masud Shah; pupil and lifelong friend of the
world's greatest mystical, lyric poet, Hafiz of Shiraz; the object of crazed
desire by (among others) Iran's greatest satirist, the obscene, outrageous,
visionary poet Obeyd Zakani; lover, then wife of womaniser Amin al-Din, a
minister of one of Persia's most loved, debauched and tragic rulers Abu
Ishak; imprisoned for twenty years under the Muzaffarids while her young
daughter mysteriously died; open-minded and scandalous, one of Iran's first
feminists ... the beautiful, petite princess who abdicated her royalty twice;
one of Iran's greatest classical lyric poets; a prolific, profound, infamous
female Persian poet...one of the greatest mystical love poets of all time
whose *Divan* is four times the size of Hafiz's. The correct rhyme-structure
is kept as well as the beauty and meaning of these beautiful, often mystical
poems. 191 pages.

KABIR: SEVEN HUNDRED SAYINGS (SAKHIS).
Translation & Introduction by Paul Smith
'Here are wonderful words of wisdom from one of the wisest of the wise.
Here are lines of love from a Master of Divine Love, and a human being
who has lived as all human beings should live, with compassion, honesty
and courage. If you want the Truth, no holds barred, it is here, but as we're
told; truth is dangerous! These poems change people. You will not be the
same! As Kabir says. "Wake up sleepy head!" ' From the Introduction
which includes a Glossary & Selected Bibliography. 188 pages.

PRINCESSES, SUFIS, DERVISHES, MARTYRS & FEMINISTS:
NINE GREAT WOMEN POETS OF THE EAST
A Selection of the Poetry of Rabi'a of Basra, Rabi'a of Balkh, Mahsati,
Lalla Ded, Jahan Khatun, Makhfi, Tahirah, Hayati and Parvin.
Introduction & Translations by Paul Smith
Rabi'a of Basra (d. 801) is considered one of the greatest Saints and
founders of Sufism and composed powerful spiritual verse in Arabic.
Rabi'a of Balkh (10th c.) was the princess of Afghanistan whose love for a
slave of her father the king caused her downfall at the hands of her mad
brother... she wrote many of her poems to her beloved in her own blood on
the walls of the prison where he tortured her to death.
Mahsati (12th century) was the liberated court poet of Sultan Sanjar who
knew Nizami, Omar Khayyam and other poets of that time. Like Omar she

only composed in the *ruba'i* form that she revolutionized with her often scandalous verse.

Lalla Ded (1320-1392) is the famous female poet/saint from Kashmir who lived at *exactly* the same time as Hafiz of Shiraz (1320-1392). Her *vakhs* (poem/sayings) are sung even today in Kashmir. She was married at a young age but the marriage was a failure and she walked out at the age of twenty-four. It must have taken a lot of courage on her part to walk around unclothed as she did. She was treated with contempt by some and much reverence by others, seeing her as a saint and eventually as God-realized. Her two hundred *vakhs* are some of the oldest examples of Kashmiri written. She was a bridge between Hindu mysticism and Sufism.

Jahan Khatun (1326-1416) was a beautiful, liberated princess in Shiraz and a friend and pupil of the great Hafiz... her *Divan* is four times the size of his. She spent 20 years in prison where her daughter died. Her *ghazals, ruba'is* and other fine poems put her in the highest rung of Persian Poets.

Makhfi or Zebunissa (1638-1702) was the daughter of the fundamentalist Emperor of India Aurangzeb and was eventually imprisoned by him and tortured to death for her Sufi views and conspiring with a brother to overthrow him. Her over 550 *ghazals* and *ruba'is* in classical Persian are deep, powerful, spiritual and at times heartbreaking.

Tahirah...(1817-1853). Tahirah was a beautiful and intelligent woman who led a short and stormy life. She became a devotee of the Bab, who from Shiraz had given his prophetic message that would later appear in the form of Baha-ul-lah, the founder of the Baha'is. She was not only a poet but also wrote prose, knew literature, religious laws and interpretations of the *Koran* and lectured... very unusual for a woman of that time and previous times in Iran. She was thirty-six when sentenced to death after the Shah was assassinated leading to a massacre of the Baha'is.

Hayati (mid 18th century - early 19th century). Bibi Hayati Kermani was born into a Sufi family in the Kerman province of Persia. She was raised by her brother, who guided her in the early stages of her spiritual life. When she was older she was initiated into the Ni'matullahi Sufi order by the Sufi Master Nur 'Ali Shah, who she was later to marry. At the request of her husband Hayati quickly composed her poetry and in her lifetime became well-known for her passionate, mystical poems that combine her great love for her husband with her devotion to Hazrat 'Ali and union with God.

Parvin...(1907-1941). Parvin E'tesami was one of Iran's greatest female poets. She learned Arabic and Persian literature from her father. She composed her first poems at eight and knew most Iranian poets by the time she was eleven, having a remarkable memory. She received a Medal of Art and Culture in 1936. Her poems had mainly social or mystical subjects, often being about the tyranny of the rich and the rights of the poor and the downtrodden and the role of women. She died in 1941 from Typhoid. The correct rhyme-structure has been kept as well as the beauty and meaning of these beautiful, sometimes mystical poems. Pages 367.

SHAH LATIF: SELECTED POEMS
Translation & Introduction by Paul Smith
Shah Abdul Latif (1689-1752) was a Sufi Master and is considered by many to be the greatest poet of the Sindhi language. His book of poetry is called the *Risalo*. His shrine is located in Bhit and attracts hundreds of pilgrims every day. He is the most famous Sindhi poet and Sufi. He was not just adored for poetry, people from far and near respected and loved him as a Spiritual Master. He composed *dohas* (self-contained strict-rhyming couplets popular with poet-saints of India like Kabir, Surdas, Tukaram) and freed it from the chain of two lines, extending it to even five or six couplets, often with irregular rhyme structures. He also introduced one more string to the *tambura*, a drone instrument and founded a new tradition in music based on the synthesis of high art and folk art. He told the basic principles of Sufism in his poetry, often using folktales about human love such as that of Sasui and Punhu, becoming a bridge to Divine Love. 172 pages

LALLA DED: SELECTED POEMS
Translation & Introduction by Paul Smith
Lalla Ded is the famous female poet/saint from Kashmir who lived at *exactly* the same time as Hafiz of Shiraz (1320-1392). Her *vakhs* (poem/sayings) are sung even today in Kashmir. She was married at a young age but the marriage was a failure and she walked out at the age of twenty-four. She became a disciple of Siddha Srikanth. It must have taken a lot of courage on her part to walk out of a marriage and to walk around unclothed as she did. She was treated with contempt by some and much reverence by others, seeing her as a saint and eventually as God-realized. Her two hundred *vakhs* are some of the oldest examples of Kashmiri written. She was a bridge between Hindu mysticism and Sufism. Her poems are more influential today than ever, not only in Kashmir but around the world. Here are 134 poems with correct form and meaning. 140 pages.

BULLEH SHAH: SELECTED POEMS
Translation & Introduction by Paul Smith
Bulleh Shah (1680-1758) was a Sufi poet who composed in Punjabi and settled in Kasur, now in Pakistan. His Spiritual Master was Shah Inayat. The poetic form Bulleh Shah is called the *Kafi*, a style of Punjabi poetry

used not only by the Sufis of Sindh and Punjab, but also by Sikh gurus. His poetry and philosophy strongly criticizes the Islamic religious orthodoxy of his day. His time was marked with communal strife between Muslims and Sikhs. But in that age Bulleh Shah was a beacon of hope and peace for the citizens of Punjab. Several of his songs or *kafis* are regarded as an integral part of the traditional repertoire of *qawwali,* the musical genre that represents the devotional music of the Sufis. The correct rhyme-structure has been kept as well as the beauty and meaning of these poems. 141 pages.

NIZAMI: MAXIMS
Translation & Introduction Paul Smith
Nizami (d. 1208) is a true Sufi Master Poet who is most famous for his six books in *masnavi* form: *The Treasury of the Mysteries, Layla and Majnun, Khrosrau and Shirin, The Seven Portraits* and his two books on Alexander. He also composed a *Divan* of approximately 20,000 couplets mostly in *ghazals* and *ruba'is...* tragically only 200 couplets survive. His influence on Attar, Rumi, Sadi, Hafiz, Jami, Shakespeare and others that followed was profound. Included in the Introduction... on the Life, Times & Poetry of Nizami includes chapters on his six *masnavis* and his *Divan,* and on the various forms of poetry he used and a Selected Bibliography. The correct rhyme-structure has been kept as well as the beauty and meaning of these wonderful two-line maxims that are not only profound, but also simple. Illustrated 214 pages.

KHIDR IN SUFI POETRY: A SELECTION
Translation & Introduction by Paul Smith
Khidr (Khizer, Khadir) is often called: "The Green One" for he was said to have drunk from the Fountain of Immortality and gained Eternal life. He has been identified with Elias, St. George, Phineas, the Angel Gabriel, the companion of Mohammed on a journey which is told in the *Koran,* viii, 59-8 1, and throughout the literature of Mysticism has appeared to many great seekers who eventually became Perfect Masters. Here are poems by many great Sufi Master Poets who have composed poems in Persian, Turkish, Pashtu, Urdu and English in which he is invoked or appears: Ansari, Anvari, Khaqani, Mu'in, Nizami, 'Attar, Baba Afzal, Rumi, Sadi, Yunus Emre, Shabistari, Amir Khusrau, Obeyd Zakani, Emad Kermani, Hafiz, Ruh Attar, Haydar, Jahan Khatun, Ahmedi, Zeyneb, Necati, Khushal, Makhfi, Rahman Baba, Khwaja Mohammad, Niyazi, Wali, Dard, Zauq, Ghalib, Dagh, Iqbal, Paul. The correct rhyme-structure has been kept as well as the beauty and meaning of these poems in various forms. Introduction on 'Who is Khidr'... Three Appendixes. Illustrated. 267 pages.

ADAM: THE FIRST PERFECT MASTER AND POET
by Paul Smith

In a series of conversations between a Master and devotees over a number of days and nights this is a long-overdue exploration and discovery and appreciation of the real spiritual status of Adam, the first God-realized human being and the first poet. Using poetry and texts of the greatest Sufi and other mystical poets this first Perfect Master's life and role is revealed and praised. The poets and Spiritual Masters include Adam Himself, Hafiz, Ibn 'Arabi, Shahin of Shiraz, 'Iraqi, Jili, Hallaj, Khushal Khan Khattak, Rumi, Ansari, Nizami, Surawadi, Mu'in ud-din Chishti, Sadi, Ibn al-Farid and Paul. The correct rhyme-structure has been kept as well as the beauty and meaning of these poems in various forms. 185 pages.

MODERN SUFI POETRY: A SELECTION
Translations & Introduction by Paul Smith

Here is one of the few anthologies of modern Sufi poetry of poets that have made a lasting impression on the present times. All the poets and Poet/Masters in this collection either died or were born in the 20th century. Most of the poets in this collection composed in the forms of earlier Sufi poets: *ghazal, ruba'i, qasida, kafi, masnavi*. Introduction: Sufis & Dervishes: Their Art and Use of Poetry, The Main Forms in Sufi and Dervish Poetry. THE POETS: Hali 47, Farid 51, Shad 57, Khusrawi 66, Iqbal 70, Munis 'Ali Shah 90, Inayat Khan 97, Asghar 122, Jigar 128, Khadim 140, Huma 151, Veysel 168, Firaq 175, Josh 185, Francis Brabazon 194, Khalili 207, Nurbaksh 214, Paul 217. Pages 249

LIFE, TIMES & POETRY OF NIZAMI
Paul Smith

Nizami (d. 1208) is a true Sufi Master Poet who is most famous for his six books in *masnavi* form: *The Treasury of the Mysteries, Layla and Majnun, Khrosrau and Shirin, The Seven Portraits* and his two books on Alexander. He also composed a *Divan* of approximately 20,000 couplets mostly in *ghazals* and *ruba'is*... tragically only 200 couplets survive. His influence on Attar, Rumi, Sadi, Hafiz and Jami and all others that followed was profound. Here a number of his *ghazals* and *ruba'is* and a *qasida* translated into English and a good selection from his *masnavis*. This book is on The Life and Times and Poetry of Nizami and on the various forms of poetry he used and the reason why he composed his major works and their effect on the times and our time. Selected Bibliography. The correct rhyme-structure has been kept as well as the beauty and meaning of the selected beautiful, mystical poems. 97 pages.

RABI'A OF BASRA: SELECTED POEMS
Translation by Paul Smith
RABI'A OF BASRA (717-801). Throughout her life, her Love of God, poverty and self-denial did not waver. She did not possess much other than a broken jug, a rush mat and a brick, which she used as a pillow. She spent nights in prayer and contemplation, chiding herself if she slept because it took her away from her active Love of God. As her fame grew she had many disciples. More interesting than her asceticism is the actual concept of Divine Love that Rabi'a introduced. She was the first to introduce the idea that God should be loved for God's own sake, not out of fear -- as earlier Sufis had done. She taught that repentance was a gift from God as none could repent unless God had already accepted him and given this gift of repentance. She had a high ideal, worshipping God neither from fear of Hell nor from hope of Paradise, for she saw such self-interest as unworthy of God's servants; emotions like fear and hope were like veils. She is widely considered the most important of the early Sufi poets. Here are most of the small number of her poems that survive, in the forms in which they were composed, also an introduction on her life and times and a chapter on Sufi poetry. 100 pages.

SATIRICAL PROSE OF OBEYD ZAKANI
Translation and Introduction by Paul Smith
Obeyd Zakani is an important a figure in Persian and Sufi literature and poetry. His satire, humorous stories, ribald and obscene poems, social commentary, mystical *ghazals*, prose, *ruba'is* and his famous epic *qasida* 'Mouse & Cat' are popular today and are more relevant than ever. He is considered to be one of the world's greatest satirist and social-commentator whose life and mystical poems had a great influence on his student and friend Hafiz and many others. Here are most of his hilarious and often obscene satirical prose works, mostly fully translated... Including his *Definitions, Joyous Treatise, The Ethics of the Nobles, The Book of the Beard* and *A Hundred Maxims*. Included is a long Introduction on his Life & Times in Shiraz and his relationship to Hafiz and the princess poet, Jahan Khatun. Selected Bibliography. 212 pages

KHAQANI: SELECTED POEMS
Translation & Introduction by Paul Smith
Born in Shirwan in 1122 he died in Tabriz in 1199. He was a great poet and a master of the *qasida* and one of the first of the *ghazal*. He was born into the family of a carpenter in Melgem, near Shamakhy. He lost his father and was brought up by an uncle, a doctor and astronomer at court of the Shirwanshah, who acted 'as his nurse and tutor'. His mother was a Christian and Jesus features in many of his poems. After he was invited to court he assumed the pen-name Khaqani ('regal'). A court poet's life bored him and he fled to Iraq inspiring his famous *masnavi* 'A Gift from the Two Iraqs'. He also wrote 'The Ruin of Madain' painting his impression of the remains of Sassanid's Palace near the Ctesiphon. Returning home Shah Akhistan ordered his imprisonment. Released he moved to Tabriz but his small son died, then daughter, then wife. Alone, he soon died. He is buried at the Poet's Cemetery in Tabriz. He left a remarkable, large heritage of poems in Persian that influenced many 'court' and Sufi poets. A major influence on his poems was Sana'i. Introduction on his Life, Poetry & Times and Forms he composed in. The correct rhyme-structure has been kept in this largest selection of his poems including *ruba'is, ghazals, masnavi, qasidas, qit'as* in English. Selected Bibliography. 195 pages.

IBN 'ARABI: SELECTED POEMS
Translation & Introduction by Paul Smith
In the West he is known as the *Doctor Maximus* and in the Islamic world as *The Great Master*. Born in Murcia in Spain in 1165 his family moved to Seville. At thirty-five he left for Mecca where he completed his most influential book of poems *The Interpreter of Ardent Desires* and began writing his masterpiece, the vast *Meccan Revelations*. In 1204 he began further travels. In 1223 he settled in Damascus where he lived the last seventeen years of his life, being executed in 1240. His tomb there is still an important place of pilgrimage. A prolific writer, Ibn 'Arabi is generally known as the prime exponent of the idea later known as the 'Unity of Being'. His emphasis was on the true potential of the human being and the path to realizing that potential and becoming the Perfect or complete person. Hundreds of works are attributed to him including a large *Divan* of poems most of which have yet to be translated. Introduction on his life and poetry. The correct rhyme-structure has been kept as well as the beauty and meaning of this selection of his beautiful, mystical poems. 121 pages.

RIBALD POEMS OF THE SUFI POETS
Sana'i, Anvari, Mahsati, Rumi, Sadi, Obeyd Zakani
Translations, Introductions Paul Smith
Some of the greatest of the Persian Sufi poets composed ribald and at times
'obscene' poems for satirical and often (as in the case of Rumi) for teaching
some spiritual truth or moral. Here is a wide-ranging selection of the
greatest of them from the eleventh to the fourteenth century. Here are at
times hilarious, witty, weird, and erotic and obscene poems in most of the
various forms of classical Persian poetry... the *ghazal,* the *ruba'i,*
the *masnavi,* the *qit'a,* the *qasida* and the *tarji-band.* 190 pages.

THE GHAZAL IN SUFI & DERVISH POETRY: An Anthology
Translations, Introductions, Etc. by Paul Smith
Introduction includes: The *Ghazal* in Arabic, Persian, Turkish, Urdu,
Punjabi, Sindhi, Pushtu, Kashmiri & English Sufi & Dervish Poetry;
Sufis & Dervishes: Their Art and Use of Poetry. Glossary of Sufi Symbols.
Included with each selection of a poet is a brief biography plus a list of
further reading. The correct rhyme-structure has been kept as well as the
beauty and meaning of these beautiful, mystical poems.
THE POETS... Hazrat Ali page 33, Rabi'a of Basra 34, Dhu'l-Nun 38,
Mansur al-Hallaj 40, Rudaki 42, Baba Kuhi 44, Sana'i 45, Khaqani 48,
Nizami 50, 'Attar 54, Kamal ud-din 65, Ibn al-Farid 66, Ibn 'Arabi 69, Rumi
74, Imami 88, Sadi 69, Iraki 118, Humam 125, Yunus Emre 127, Amir
Khusraw 138, Hasan Dihlavi 148, Auhadi 150, Ibn Yamin 152, Khaju 153,
Obeyd Zakani 158, Emad 167, Hafiz 176, Ruh Attar 213, Ahmedi 218,
Haydar 222, Junaid Shirazi 226, Kadi Burhan-ud-din 230, Jahan Khatun 233,
Kamal 252, Maghribi 255, Nesimi 264, Sheykhi 273, Kasim Anwar 276, Shah
Ni'matu'llah 280, Jami 281, Baba Fighani 293, Pir Sultan 298, Khayali 302,
Fuzuli 308, Huda'i 317, Qutub Shah 325, Mirza 327, Sa'ib 337, Khushal 340,
Ashraf Khan 349, Makhfi 354, Bedil 385, Abdul-Khadir 389, Rahman Baba
395, Khwaja Mohammad 409, Hamid 419, Niyazi 428, Wali 430, Mushtaq
434, Ali Haider 436, Sauda 437, Dard 439, Nazir 455, Mir 462, Sachal
Sarmast 468, Galib 473, Esrar Dede 479, Aatish 481, Zauq 484, Tahirah 487,
Shad 491, Iqbal 495, Ashgar 500, Jigar 503, Huma 508, Veysel 532, Paul 536.
Pages 560.

MAKHFI: THE PRINCESS SUFI POET ZEB-UN-NISSA
A Selection of Poems from her *Divan*
Translation & Introduction by Paul Smith
Makhfi (1638-1702) pen-name meaning 'concealed', was Zeb-un-Nissa the
beautiful and talented oldest daughter of the strict Muslim Emperor of
India, Aurangzeb. She was imprisoned for 20 years for her Sufi views and
conspiring with a brother against him. Her over 550 *ghazals* and *ruba'is* in
Persian are deep, spiritual and at times truly heartbreaking.
The correct forms and spiritual meaning are preserved in this large selection
of her poetry. Selected Bibliography. 126 pages.

~THE SUFI RUBA'IYAT~A Treasury of Sufi and Dervish Poetry
in the Ruba'i form, from Rudaki to the 21st Century
Translations, Introductions, Notes etc. by Paul Smith
Introduction includes...Sufis & Dervishes: Their Art and Use of Poetry...
The Form of the *Ruba'i* in Persian, Arabic, Turkish, Urdu & English Sufi &
Dervish Poetry & a Glossary. Included with each selection of a particular
poet is a brief biography plus a list of further reading. The correct rhyme-
structure has been kept as well as the beauty and meaning of these beautiful,
mystical poems. THE POETS...Rudaki page 31, Mansur al-Hallaj 34,
Shibli 36, Baba Tahir 37, Abu Said 42, Ibn Sina 48, Baba Kuhi 51, Ansari 52,
Al-Ghazzali 54, Hamadani 56, Sana'i 58, Mahsati 62, Khaqani 66, Nizami
70, Ruzbihan 72, Baghdadi 74, 'Attar 76, Auhad-ud-din Kermani 83, Kamal
ud-din 87, Hamavi 91, Baba Afzal 93, Rumi 96, Imami 106, Sadi 107, Iraki
112, Sultan Valad 117, Humam 119, Amir Khusraw 121, Simnani 125, Ibn
Yamin 127, Khaju 128, Obeyd Zakani 130, Emad 132, Hafiz 133, Ruh Attar
141, Kadi Burhan-ud-din 142, Jahan Khatun 144, Kamal 152, Maghribi 152,
Nesimi 155, Kasim Anwar 158, Shah Ni'matu'llah 159, Jami 162, Baba
Fighani 165, Fuzuli 166, Ghazali 168, Urfi 170, Qutub Shah 172, Haleti 174,
Dara Shikoh 176, Sarmad 179, Sa'ib 189, Nasir Ali 190, Makhfi 191, Bedil
194, Mushtaq 188, Sauda 200, Dard 203, Esrar Dede 205, Hatif 206, Mir 208,
Aatish 211, Zauq 213, Dabir 215, Anees 216, Hali 218, Shad 220, Iqbal 222,
Khalili 225, Rahi 229, Nurbakhsh, Paul 232.   Pages... 244.

RUBAI'YAT OF THE WORLD: An Anthology
Court, Sufi, Dervish, Satirical, Ribald, Prison and Social Poetry in the
Ruba'i form from the 9th to the 20th century from the Arabic, Persian,
Turkish and Urdu
Translations, Introduction and Notes by Paul Smith
Introduction includes chapter on the *ruba'i*. Included with each selection of a

particular poet is a brief biography plus a list of further reading. The correct rhyme-structure has been kept as well as the beauty and meaning of these beautiful, often mystical poems.

THE POETS... Hanzalah page 11, Mansur-al Hallaj 12, Shibli 15, Abu Shakur 16, Shahid 17, Rudaki 18, Rabi'a Balkhi 122, Daqiqi 24, Umarah 27, Firdausi 28, Baba Tahir 31, Farrukhi 36, Asjadi 38, Unsuri 39, Abu Said 42, Ibn Sina 49, Baba Kuhi 52, Azraqi 54, Qatran 56, Ansari 58, Al-Ghazali 61, Mas'ud Sad 63, Mu'izzi 68, Hamadani 71, Omar Khayyam 74, Sana'i 77, Sabir 82, Mahsati 83, Jabali 93, Vatvat 95, Anvari 98, Khaqani 103, Zahir 108, Nizami 111, Ruzbihan 113, Baghdadi 115, 'Attar 118, Auhad ud-din Kermani 126, Kamal ad-din 132, Hamavi 136, Baba Afzal 139, Rumi 142, Imami 153, Hamgar 154, Sadi 158, Iraki 165, Sultan Valad 161, Humam 173, Amir Khusraw 176, Simnani 180, Ibn Yamin 183, Khaju 185, Obeyd Zakani 188, Emad 193, Salman 195, Hafiz 197, Ruh Attar 206, Kadi Burhan-ud-din 208, Jahan Khatun 210, Shah Shuja 220, Kamal 223, Maghribi 224, Bushaq 227, Kasim Anwar 232, Shah Ni'tmu'llah 234, Nesimi 237, Jami 241, Nejati 244, Baba Fighani 246, Babur 248, Humayan 251, Kamran 254, Fuzuli 256, Ghazali 254, Kahi 257, Akbar 258, Urfi 260, Hayati 263, Ulfati 264, Qutub Shah 269, Haleti 271, Dara Shikoh 274, Sarmad 277, Sa'ib 285, Nasir Ali 287, Makhfi 289, Nabi 292, Bedil 294, Nedim 300, Mushtaq 302, Sauda 305. Dard 308, Esrar Dede 311, Nishat 313, Hatif 315, Mir 317, Aatish 321, Zauq 323, Ghalib 325, Momin 329, Dabir 332, Anees 334, Hali 337, Akbar Allahbadi 339, Shad 341, Iqbal 343, Mehroom 347, Firaq 349, Josh 352, Khalili 357, Rahi 361, Faiz, Nurbaksh 364. Pages 367.

LOVE'S AGONY & BLISS: ANTHOLOGY OF URDU POETRY
Sufi, Dervish, Court and Social Poetry from the 16th-20th Century
Translations, Introductions, Etc. by Paul Smith

Introduction includes...The Urdu Language, Urdu Poetry, The *Ghazal* in Urdu Poetry, *Ghazal* Singing in India & Pakistan, The *Ruba'i* in Urdu Poetry, The *Masnavi* in Urdu Poetry, Glossary for Sufi & Dervish Urdu Poetry. Included with each selection of a particular poet is a brief biography plus a list of further reading. The correct rhyme-structure has been kept as well as the beauty and meaning of these beautiful, often mystical poems.

THE POETS...Qutub Shah page 29, Wali 34, Sauda 43, Dard 51, Nazir 60, Mir 74, Aatish 96, Zauq 107, Ghalib 114, Momin 130, Dabir 138, Anees 142, Hali 146, Akbar Allahabadi 150, Shad 152, Iqbal 160, Asghar 170, Mehroom 175, Josh 177, Jigar 187, Huma 196, Firaq 216, Faiz 228. Pages 230.

BREEZES OF TRUTH
Selected Early & Classical Arabic Sufi Poetry
Translations, Introductions, Etc., by Paul Smith
Introduction includes...Sufis: Their Art and Use of Poetry & The Main
Forms in Arabic Sufi Poetry.
Included with each selection of a particular poet is a brief biography plus a
list of further reading. The correct rhyme-structure has been kept as well as
the beauty and meaning of these beautiful, mystical poems.
THE POETS... Hazrat Ali page 19, Ali Ibn Husain 21, Rabi'a of Basra 23,
Dhu'l-Nun 36, Bayazid Bistami 47, Al Nuri 50, Junaid 44, Sumnun 65,
Mansur al-Hallaj 71, Shibli 101, Ibn Sina 111, Al-Ghazzali 114, Gilani 118,
Suhrawadi 122, Ibn al-Farid 129, Ibn 'Arabi 143. Pages 185.

THE~DIVINE~WINE : A Treasury of Sufi and Dervish Poetry
(Volume One)
Translations, Introductions, Etc. by Paul Smith
Introduction includes...Sufis & Dervishes: Their Art and Use of Poetry,
The Main Forms in Arabic, Persian, Turkish, Kashmiri, Hindi, Urdu,
Punjabi, Sindhi & English Sufi & Dervish Poetry. Glossary of Sufi &
Dervish Symbols. Included with each selection of a particular poet is a brief
biography plus a list of further reading. The correct rhyme-structure has
been kept as well as the beauty and meaning of these beautiful, mystical
poems.
THE POETS... Hazrat Ali page 39, Ali Ibn Husain 40, Rabi'a of Basra
40, Dhu'l-Nun 46, Bayazid Bistami 53, Al Nuri 54, Junaid 57, Sumnun 59,
Mansur al-Hallaj 60, Rudaki 67, Shibli 72, Baba Tahir 74, Abu Said 78, Ibn
Sina 85, Baba Kuhi 88, Ansari 90, Al-Ghazzali 92, Hamadani 95, Sana'i 98,
Gilani 109, Mahsati 112, Khaqani 117, Suhrawadi 122, Nizami 126, Ruzbihan
150, Baghdadi 152, 'Attar 154, Auhad-ud-din Kermani 177, Kamal ud-din 182,
Ibn al-Farid 186, Ibn 'Arabi 197, Baba Farid 206, Hamavi 213, Baba Afzal
216, Rumi 218, Imami 269, Sadi 271, Iraki 341, Sultan Valad 352, Humam 358,
Yunus Emre 362, Amir Khusraw 375, Hasan Dihlavi 386, Simnani 388,
Auhadi 391, Ibn Yamin 395, Khaju 398, Obeyd Zakani 404, Emad 417, Lalla
Ded 426, Hafiz 429, Jahan Khatun 490.   Pages 550.

THE~DIVINE~WINE: A Treasury of Sufi and Dervish Poetry
(Volume Two)
Translations, Introductions, Etc. by Paul Smith
Introduction includes...Sufis & Dervishes: Their Art and Use of Poetry...
The Main Forms in Arabic, Persian, Turkish, Kashmiri, Hindi, Urdu,

Punjabi, Pusthu, Sindhi & English Sufi & Dervish Poetry. Glossary of Sufi Symbols. The correct rhyme-structure has been kept as well as the beauty and meaning of these beautiful, mystical poems.

Included with each poet is a brief biography plus a list of further reading.

THE POETS: Ruh Attar page 39, Haydar 47, Junaid Shirazi 58, Ahmedi 62, Kadi Burhan-ud-din 66, Kamal 70, Maghribi 74, Nesimi 83, Sheykhi 95, Kasim Anwar 97, Shah Ni'matu'llah 104, Kabir 110, Jami 125, Fighani 141, Pir Sultan 147, Khayali 150, Fuzuli 156, Huda'i 167, Urfi 169, Qutub Shah 173, Mirza 176, Nef'i 190, Sa'ib 197, Dara Shikoh 200, Sarmad 202, Khushal 212, Sultan Bahu 221, Ashraf Khan 226, Nasir Ali 231, Makhfi 232, Bedil 265, Abdul-Khan 273, Rahman Baba 279, Khwaja Mohammad 296, Hamid 305, Niyazi 316, Wali 319, Bulleh Shah 323, Shah Latif 329, Mushtaq 337, Ali Haider 341, Sauda 343, Dard 347, Ahmad Shah 351, Shaida 358, Nazir 364, Hatif 377, Mir 384, Sachal Sarmast 395, Galib 400, Esrar Dede 406, Aatish 409, Zauq 413, Dabir 416, Anees 418, Tahirah 420, Hali 429, Farid 431, Shad 433, Iqbal 438, Inayat Khan 448, Ashgar 463, Jigar 465, Huma 470, Veysel 498, Firaq 501, Josh 506, Brabazon 510, Khalili 518, Nurbaksh 522, Paul 524. Pages 556.

TONGUES ON FIRE: An Anthology of the Sufi, Dervish, Warrior & Court Poetry of Afghanistan.
Translations, Introductions, Etc. by Paul Smith
Introduction includes… The Main Forms in Dari/Persian, and Pushtu Poetry; Sufis & Dervishes: Their Art and Use of Poetry. Glossary.
Included with each selection of a particular poet is a brief biography plus a list of further reading. The correct rhyme-structure has been kept as well as the beauty and meaning of these beautiful and mainly mystical poems.
THE POETS… Hanzalah page 19, Abu Shakur 21, Shahid 24, Rudaki 27, Rabai'a Balkhi 38, Daqiqi 47, Nasir-i-Khusraw 55, Ansari 59, Azraqi 63, Sana'i 66, Zahir 81, Rumi 96, Imami 151, Jami 155, Mirza 176, Khushal 194, Ashraf Khan 212, Bedil 219, Abdul-Kadir 229, Rahman Baba 237, Khwaja Mohammad 257, Hamid 270, Ahmad Shah 287, Shaida 297, Khalili 303. 325 pages.

THE SEVEN GOLDEN ODES (QASIDAS) OF ARABIA (The Mu'allaqat)
Translations, Introduction & Notes by Paul Smith
The Mu'allaqat is the title of a group of seven long Arabic odes or qasidas that have come down from the time before Islam. Each is considered the best work of these pre-Islamic poets. The name means 'The Suspended Qasidas'

or 'The Hanging Poems', the traditional explanation being that these poems
were hung on or in the Kaaba at Mecca.

These famous ancient Arabic *qasidas* are formed of three parts: they start,
with a nostalgic opening in which the poet reflects on what has passed,
known as *nasib*. A common concept is the pursuit of the poet of the caravan
of his love; by the time he reaches their campsite they have already moved
on. The second section is *rahil* (travel section) in which the poet
contemplates the harshness of nature and life away from the tribe. Finally
there is the message of the poem, which can take several forms: praise of the
tribe, *fakhr;* satire about other tribes, *hija;* or some moral maxims, *hikam.*
Included with each *qasida* of each poet is a brief biography plus a list of
further reading. The correct rhyme-structure has been kept as well as the
beauty and meaning of these beautiful poems.

CONTENTS: The Introduction... The *Mu'allaqat* 7, The *Qasida* 17.
The Poets... Imra'ul-Qays 19, Tarafa 37, Amru 59, Harith 73, Antara 83,
Zuhair 103, Labid 119. Appendix... Kab's *Qasida* of the Mantle 139.
Pages... 140.

THE QASIDA: A WORLD ANTHOLOGY
Translations, Introduction & Notes by Paul Smith

The *qasida* is a form of praise poetry from pre-Islamic Arabia. It sometimes
runs to more than 50 lines and sometimes more than 100. It was later
inherited by the Persians, the Turks, the Afghans and Urdu Poets where it
was developed immensely by Sufi, court and tribal poets. The *qasida*
resembles a *ghazal* in many ways except that it is longer. In the first
couplet, both the lines rhyme, and the same rhyme runs through the whole
poem, the rhyme-word being at the end of the second line of each couplet
(after the first couplet).

Included with each selection of a particular poet is a brief biography plus a
list of further reading. The correct rhyme-structure has been kept as well as
the beauty and meaning of these beautiful poems.

CONTENTS: Introduction: The *Qasida:* The Beginnings in Arabia...
The Persian *Qasida*... *Qasida* in Turkey.

THE POETS (In Order of Appearance) Imra' ul-Qays 13, Tarafa 25, Amru
39, Harith 48, Antara 55, Zuhair 68, Labid 78, Ka'b 90, Rudaki 28, Dhu'l-
Nun 99, Kisa'i 104, Farrukhi 106, Minuchirhri 114, Unsuri 119, Ibn Sina 123,
Nasir-i-Khusraw 125, Al-Ghazali 128, Asadi 131, Azraqi 137, Qatran 139,
Mas'ud Sad 143, Mu'izzi 149, Sana'i 154, Jabali 159, Gilani 162, Anvari 165,
Falaki 169, Khaqani 172, Abu Madyan 178, Suhrawardi 183, Zahir 187,
Nizami 193, Ibn al-Farid 197, Ibn 'Arabi 209, Hamgar 213, Iraki 215, Humam
218, Amir Khusraw 220, Auhadi 224, Obeyd Zakani 226, Salman 234, Hafiz

239, Ruh Attar 255, Haydar 259, Azad 267, Shah Shuja 269, Shah
Ni'tmu'llah 272, Necati 276, Fuzuli 282, Baqi 285, Urfi 290, Mirza 292, Nef'i
298, Niyazi 301, Khushal 304, Rahman Baba 310, Hamid 314, Ghalib 317,
Parvin 322, Paul 328.   407 pages.

IBN AL-FARID: WINE & THE MYSTIC'S PROGRESS
Translation, Introduction & Notes by Paul Smith
Umar Ibn al-Farid, an Egyptian poet (1181-1235), is considered to be the
undisputed master of Islamic mystical poetry into Arabic. He is considered
not only to be a poet but a Perfect Master (Qutub) a God-realised soul...
and it is his journey to unity with God that he reveals in probably the
longest qasida (ode) in Arabic (761 couplets), his famous The Mystic's
Progress. The other poem for which he is most known is his Wine Poem that
is often seen as a prologue to the The Mystic's Progress.
Although these long poems have been translated into English before this is
the first time in the correct rhyme of the qasida and in clear, concise, modern
English. Included in the Introduction are chapters on his Life & Work, The
Qasida in Arabic, Previous Qasidas by Master Arab Poets that would have
influenced him, The Perfect Master (Qutub), and the Wine Poem and The
Mystic's Way. Selected Bibliography. The correct rhyme-structure has been
kept as well as the beauty and meaning of these beautiful poems. Appendix
upon the other translations into English of both poems. 174 pages.

RUBA'IYAT OF ABU SA'ID
Translation. Introduction & Notes by Paul Smith.
Abu Sa'id ibn Abi 'l-Khair (968-1049) was a Perfect Master and a poet who
lived in Nishapur and composed only ruba'is, over 400 of them. He was a
founder of Sufi poetry and a major influence on the ruba'i and most poets
that followed, especially Sana'i, Nizami, 'Attar, Rumi and Hafiz. Here are
188 of his poems translated into the correct form. Included in Introduction is
the life of Abu Sa'id and a history of the ruba'i and examples by its greatest
exponents. Bibliography. The correct rhyme-structure is kept as well as the
beauty and meaning of these immortal four-line poems. 227 pages.

RUBA'IYAT OF BABA TAHIR
Translations, Introduction & Notes by Paul Smith
Baba Tahir, or Oryan ('The Naked') of Hamadan... approx. 990-1065, was
a great God-intoxicated, or God-mad soul (mast) and possibly a Qutub
(Perfect Master) who composed about 120 known ruba'i in a simpler metre
than the usual 'hazaj' metre. His simple, mystical poems that he would sing
while wandering naked throughout the land had a profound influence on

Sufis and dervishes and other *ruba'i* composers, especially Abu Sa'id, Ibn Sina and Omar Khayyam. Included in the Introduction is the life of Baba Tahir and a history of the *ruba'i* and examples by its greatest exponents. Selected Bibliography. The correct rhyme-structure has been kept as well as the beauty and meaning of these immortal four-line poems. 154 pages.

THE POETS OF SHIRAZ
Sufi, Dervish, Court & Satirical Poets from the 9th to the 20th Centuries of the fabled city of Shiraz
Translations & Introduction & Notes by Paul Smith
CONTENTS: Shiraz in History. The Various Forms in Classical Persian Poetry, Sufism in Persian Poetry, A Glossary of Sufi & Dervish Poetry THE POETS OF SHIRAZ... 49 Mansur al-Hallaj 51, Baba Kuhi 59, Ruzbihan 59, Hamgar 65, Sadi 70, Nasir 123, Khaju 127, Obeyd Zakani 136, Emad 187, Shahin 199, Hafiz 218, Ruh Attar 299, Haydar 313, Yazdi 326, Azad 328, Junaid 332, Jalal 336, Jahan Khatun 337, Shah Shuja 381, Bushaq 387, Shah Da'i, 400, Ahli 407, Figani 409, Urfi 414, Visal 419, Qa'ani 420, Shurida 427, Munis 'Ali Shah 429, Lotfali Suratgar 433, Mehdi Hamidi 436. 436 pages.

RUBA'IYAT OF 'ATTAR
Translation, Introduction & Notes by Paul Smith
Farid ad-din 'Attar (d. 1221) is the Perfect Master Poet who was the author of over forty books of poetry and prose including *The Conference of the Birds, The Book of God* (which he is said to have presented to Rumi when he met him) and *The Lives of the Saints.* Apart from his many books in *masnavi* form he also composed many hundreds of mystical *ghazals* and *ruba'is.* He also changed the evolution of the *ruba'i* form by composing a long Sufi epic, the *Mukhtar-nama,* where each of 2088 *ruba'is* is connected by subject matter that Fitzgerald attempted to do with those he attributed to Omar Khayyam.
Included in the Introduction is the life of 'Attar and a history of the *ruba'i* and examples by its greatest exponents. Selected Bibliography. The correct rhyme-structure has been kept as well as the beauty and meaning of these immortal four-line poems. 114 Pages.

RUBA'IYAT OF MAHSATI
Translation, Introduction & Notes by Paul Smith
We know little of Mahsati Ganjavi's life (1098-1185) except that she lived in Ganjeh where Sultan Sanjar reigned and as she was a poet at his court she would have known Anvari. She was a court, dervish and ribald poet. She

knew Nizami (she is said to have been buried in his mausoleum) and Omar Khayyam… and like Omar composed only in the *ruba'i* form and must be considered not only a master of that form but also to have helped revolutionize it. She was an influence on perhaps Iran's greatest female poet Jahan Khatun of Shiraz and Iran's greatest satirist Obeyd Zakani. She was famous and also infamous for her liberated behaviour. Included in the Introduction are the life of Mahsati and a history of the *ruba'i* and examples by its greatest exponents. Selected Bibliography. The correct rhyme-structure has been kept as well as the beauty and meaning of these immortal four-line poems. 144 Pages.

RUBA'IYAT OF JAHAN KHATUN
Translation by Paul Smith & Rezvaneh Pashai
Introduction & Notes by Paul Smith
Jahan Khatun (1326-1416?) was the daughter of the king of one of Shiraz's most turbulent times… Masud Shah; pupil and lifelong friend of the world's greatest mystical, lyric poet, Hafiz of Shiraz; the object of crazed desire by (among others) Iran's greatest satirist, the obscene, outrageous, visionary poet Obeyd Zakani; lover, then wife of womanizer Amin al-Din, a minister of one of Persia's most loved, debauched and tragic rulers… Abu Ishak. She was cruelly imprisoned for twenty years under the Muzaffarids while her young daughter mysteriously died; open-minded and scandalous, one of Iran's first feminists… the beautiful and sensuous, petite princess who abdicated her royalty twice is one of Iran's greatest classical lyric poets whose *Divan* is four times larger than that of Hafiz's and contains about 2000 *ghazals* and many hundreds of wonderful *ruba'is*. Included in the Introduction is the life of Jahan and a history of the *ruba'i* and examples by its greatest exponents. Selected Bibliography. The correct rhyme-structure has been kept as well as the beauty and meaning of these immortal four-line poems. 157 Pages.

RUBA'IYAT OF SANA'I
Translation, Introduction & Notes by Paul Smith
One of the most prolific and influential Sufi Master Poets of all time Hakim Sana'i (d.1131) composed many *ghazals, masnavis* and <u>over 400</u> *ruba'is* that influenced all the *ruba'i* writers that followed him, especially Mahsati and 'Attar. His long *masnavi* (rhyming couplets) mystical work *The Enclosed Garden of the Truth* is said to have had a profound influence on Rumi's composing of his *Masnavi* and in Sadi's composing his *Bustan* ('The Orchard'). Included in the Introduction are the life of Sana'i and a history of the *ruba'i* and examples by its greatest exponents. Selected

Bibliography. The correct rhyme-structure has been kept as well as the beauty and meaning of these immortal four-line poems. 111 Pages.

RUBA'IYAT OF JAMI
Translation, Introduction & Notes by Paul Smith
Jami (1414-1493), considered the last great poet of the Classical Period (10th-15thC.) is mostly known for his masterpiece seven *masnavis* epics… including *Joseph and Zulaikh, Layla and Majnun,* and *Salman and Absal.* He also composed three *Divans* consisting of *ghazals rubai's* and other profound mystical poems. Here are 103 *ruba'is,* the largest number ever put into English. Included in the Introduction are the life of Jami and a history of the *ruba'i* and examples by its greatest exponents. Selected Bibliography. The correct rhyme-structure has been kept as well as the beauty and meaning of these beautiful, mystical four-line poems. 178 Pages.

RUBA'IYAT OF SARMAD
Translation, Introduction & Notes by Paul Smith
Sarmad (d. 1659) or Hazrat Sarmad Shaheed, whose name 'Sarmad' derives from the Persian word for eternal or everlasting, was a famous and infamous Persian dervish poet of Jewish and Armenian origin. As a merchant he gathered his wares and travelled to India to sell them. In India he renounced Judaism and adopted Islam: he later renounced it in favour of Hinduism which he finally renounced for Sufism. He was known for exposing and ridiculing the major religions and hypocrisy of his day, but he also wrote beautiful mystical poetry in the form of 321 *rubai's* (all here translated). He wandered the streets and the courts of the emperor as a naked dervish. He was beheaded in 1659 by Emperor Aurangzeb for his perceived heretical poetry. His grave is located near the Jama Masjid in Delhi. 381 pages.

RUBA'IYAT OF HAFIZ
Translation, Introduction & Notes by Paul Smith
Persia's greatest exponent of the *ghazal* Hafiz (1320-1392) became a Perfect Master *(Qutub),* was twice exiled from his beloved Shiraz for his criticism of rulers and false Sufi masters and hypocritical clergy. His *Divan* shows he composed in other forms including the *ruba'i* of which about 160 survive. As with his *ghazals,* his *ruba'is* are sometimes mystical and sometimes critical of the hypocrisy of his times. Included in the Introduction is the life of Hafiz and a history of the *ruba'i* and examples by its greatest exponents. Selected Bibliography. The correct rhyme-structure has been kept as well as the beauty and meaning of these immortal four-line poems. 220 Pages.

YUNUS EMRE, THE TURKISH DERVISH: SELECTED POEMS
Translation, Introduction & Notes by Paul Smith

Yunus Emre (d. 1320) is considered one of the most important Turkish poets having a great influence on Turkish literature from his own time until today. His poems concern divine love as well as human love of the Divine as God and the Perfect Master, Beloved, Friend and human destiny and weakness. Little is known of his life other than he became a Sufi dervish Perfect Master (*Qutub*). A contemporary of Rumi, it is told the two great souls met: Rumi asked Yunus what he thought of his huge work, the *Mesnevi*. Yunus said, "Excellent! But I would have done it differently." Surprised, Rumi asked how. Yunus replied, "I'd have written, 'I came from the eternal, clothed myself in flesh, took the name Yunus.'" This illustrates his simple approach that has made him loved by many. His poems were probably a great influence on Hafiz who was born the year he died and who knew Turkish. Here is the largest selection of his poems translated into English mainly in the form of the *gazel* that he often used. The correct rhyme-structure has been kept as well as the beauty and meaning of these beautiful, mystical poems.

Included... an Introduction on his Life & Times and the Form and History & Function of the *gazel* and a chapter on Sufism & Poetry, Turkish Poetry and the Turkish Language and a Selected Bibliography. Pages... 237

RUBA'IYAT OF KAMAL AD-DIN
Translation, Introduction & Notes by Paul Smith

Kamal ad-din Isma'il (1172-1238) known as 'The Creator of Subtle Thoughts' was the son of the court poet Jamal ad-din and was one of the last of the great poets of the early days in Isfahan. Both father and son praised their city and the same patrons but Kamal ad-din considered himself not only a court poet but a Sufi or Dervish. His *qasidas* in the style of Iraki were greatly admired and some were said to 'reach the summit of perfection' but it is his many much loved human and divine *ruba'is* that his fame now rests upon. Here are the largest number of his *ruba'is* ever put into English.

Included in the Introduction... the Life and Times of Kamal ad-din and a history of the *ruba'i* and examples by its greatest exponents and a chapter on Sufi Poetry. The correct rhyme-structure has been kept and the beauty and meaning of these beautiful, mystical, loving, sometimes satirical four-line poems. Pages 152.

RUBA'YAT OF KHAYYAM
Translation, Introduction & Notes by Paul Smith
Reprint of 1909 Introduction by R.A. Nicholson

Of the 900 to 2000 or so *ruba'is* attributed to Omar Khayyam (died 1132) over 500 years only about ten to twenty percent are now considered to be his. More famous in Iran as an astronomer and mathematician... his nihilistic and hedonistic and occasionally Sufi philosophy in his *ruba'is* meant that his poems were never really popular in his homeland, but of course after the work of FitzGerald the west fell in love with him. Included in the Introduction... the Life and Times of Omar Khayyam and his work as a Scientist & Philosopher and a history of the *ruba'i* and examples by its greatest exponents and a chapter on the various translations into English and other languages. Selected bibliography. The correct rhyme-structure has been kept as well as the beauty and meaning of these beautiful, fatalistic, intoxicated, loving, sometimes mystical and satirical 186 four-line poems. 266 pages.

RUBA'IYAT OF AUHAD UD-DIN
Translation and Introduction by Paul Smith
Auhad ud-din Kermani (1164-1238) was influenced by 'Attar, Ibn 'Arabi (whom he knew) and Suhrawadi and was a powerful speaker and a Sufi Master whose disciples at one time numbered over 70,000.
He used the *ruba'i* form (composing over 1700) in his teaching although he also composed in other forms. Among his followers was Auhadi of Maragha who took his *takhallus* or pen-name from his master. His ideas and behaviour was said to have shocked many of his fellow Sufis and contemporaries. Included in the Introduction... the Life and Work of Auhad ud-din and a history of the *ruba'i* and examples by its greatest exponents and a chapter on Sufi Poetry. The correct rhyme-structure has been kept as well as the beauty and meaning of these mystical, loving four-line poems. 109 pages.

HUMA: SELECTED POEMS OF MEHER BABA
Translation & Introduction by Paul Smith
Merwan S. Irani (1894-1969), known world-wide as Meher Baba, took Huma (Phoenix) as his *takhallus* or pen-name when he composed enlightened *ghazals* in a mixture of Persian, Urdu and Gujarati in his twenties as a realized disciple of the *Qutub* or Perfect Master Upasni Maharaj, and also later on. He knew the *ghazals* of Hafiz by heart as did his father, the dervish Sheriar Irani, who had originally walked to Pune in India from Khooramshah in Iran. Merwan went on to reveal himself as *Qutub* and later also declared himself as the *Rasool* or Messiah (Avatar). The correct rhyme-structure has been kept as well as the beauty and meaning of these beautiful, mystical poems. Contents: The Life of Meher

Baba... page 7, The *Ghazal,* its Form and History 21, Selected Bibliography 27 *Ghazals* 29, *Qit'as* (Fragments), 83. Pages... 116.

RUBA'IYAT OF AL-MA'ARRI
Translation & Introduction by Paul Smith
CONTENTS: The Life and Works of al Ma'arri... Page 7 Selected Bibliography... 14, The *Ruba'i:* Its Form, Use and History... 15, Ruba'iyat of al-Ma'arri... 31.
Abu'l- 'Ala al-Ma'arri was born in Ma'arra, south of Aleppo in Syria in 973 A.D. He achieved fame as one of greatest of Arab poets. Al-Ma'arri was stricken with smallpox when four and became blind. His early poems in *ruba'i* form gained great popularity. As he grew older, he was able to travel to Aleppo, Antioch and other Syrian cities. Al-Ma'arri spent 18 months at Baghdad, then the centre of learning and poetry, leaving to return to his native town. There he created the *Luzumiyyat,* a famous collection of 1592 poems. On return, his presence in al-Ma'arra drew many people, who came to hear him lecture on poetry and rhetoric. 128 pages.

ANTHOLOGY OF CLASSICAL ARABIC POETRY (From Pre-Islamic Times to Ibn 'Arabi)
Translations, Introduction and Notes by Paul Smith
CONTENTS: Classical Arabic Poetry... page 7, The Qasida... 10, The Qit'a... 11, The Ghazal... 12, The Ruba'i... 16, Selected Bibliography... 17: THE POETS (In Order of Appearance) Imra' ul-Qays 19, Zuhair 31, Harith 41, Antara 48, Tarafa 62, Amru 76, Al-A'sha 86, Suhaym 88, Labid 90, Ka'b 102, Khansa 107, Hazrat Ali 109, Ali Ibn Husain 111, Omar Ibn Abi Rabi'a 113, Majnun 116, Rab'ia of Basra 123, Bashshar 130, Abu Nuwas 133, Abu Tammam 153, Dhu'l-Nun 157, Bayazid Bistami 165, Al-Nuri 167, Junaid 171, Sumnun 173, Mansur al-Hallaj 175, Al-Mutanabbi 184, Al-Ma'arri 212, Ibn Sina 230, Al-Ghazali 233, Gilani 236, Abu Madyan 240, Suhrawardi 245, Ibn al-Farid 249, Ibn 'Arabi 262. Pages 272.

THE QIT'A: Anthology of the 'Fragment' in Arabic, Persian and Eastern Poetry.
Translations, Introduction and Notes by Paul Smith
Contents: Arabic Poetry... page 7, Persian Poetry... 10 The Form & Function of the Qit'a... 12 .THE POETS (In Order of Appearance) Al-A'sha 15, Khansa 17, Omar Ibn Abi Rabi'a 19, Suhaym 22, Ali Ibn Husain 24, Raba'i of Basra 26, Majnun 32, Bashshar 40, Abu Nuwas 43, Abu Tammam 63, Abbas of Merv 67, Hanzalah 69, Firuz 71, Dhu'l-Nun 73, Bayazid Bistami 76, Al-Nuri 78, Junaid 82, Sumnun 84, Mansur al-Hallaj

HEARTS WITH WINGS Anthology of Persian Sufi and Dervish Poetry
Translations, Introductions, Etc., by Paul Smith
CONTENTS: Introduction...Persian Poetry: A New Beginning... Sufis & Dervishes: Their Art and Use of Poetry... The Main Forms in Persian Sufi & Dervish Poetry... Glossary.
Included with each selection of a particular poet is a brief biography plus a list of further reading. The correct rhyme-structure has been kept as well as the beauty and meaning of these beautiful, mystical poems.

HAFIZ: SELECTED POEMS
Translation, Introduction & Notes by Paul Smith
Persia's greatest exponent of the *ghazal* Hafiz (1320-1390) became a Perfect Master *(Qutub)*, was twice exiled from his beloved Shiraz for his criticism of rulers and false Sufi masters and hypocritical clergy. His *Divan* shows he composed in nearly all forms. As with his *ghazals,* his *masnavis, qasidas, qita's, ruba'is* and other poems are sometimes mystical and sometimes critical of the hypocrisy of his times. Included in the Introduction is the Life

and Times and Poetry of Hafiz and a history of the various forms. Selected Bibliography. Glossary. The correct rhyme-structure has been kept as well as the beauty and meaning of these immortal four-line poems. 227 Pages.

'ATTAR: SELECTED POETRY
Translation, Introduction & Notes by Paul Smith
Farid ad-din 'Attar is seen with Sana'i and Rumi (who he met and influenced) as one of the three most important Sufi Poet –Masters of the 13th century. He composed over forty books mainly in the epic *masnavi* form of rhyming couplets, his most famous being *The Book of God* and The *Conference of the Birds*. He also composed many powerful mystical poems in the *ghazal* form and in the *ruba'i* form. Here for the first time is a fine selection of his poems in all three forms in the correct-rhyme structure with the beauty and meaning of his immortal poems. Introduction on his Life & Times and Poetry and an essay by Inayat Khan on Sufi Poetry. Selected Bibliography & Glossary. 177 pages.

SANA'I: SELECTED POEMS
Translation, Introduction & Notes by Paul Smith
One of the most prolific and influential Sufi Master Poets of all time Hakim Sana'i (d.1131) composed many *ghazals, masnavis, qasidas, qita's* and over 400 *ruba'is* that influenced all the *ruba'i* writers that followed him. His long *masnavi* (rhyming couplets) mystical work *The Enclosed Garden of the Truth* is said to have had a profound influence on Rumi's composing of his *Masnavi* and in Sadi's composing his *Bustan* ('The Orchard'). Included in the Introduction are the Life and Times and Poetry of Sana'i and a history of the various poetic forms that he wrote in. Selected Bibliography. The correct rhyme-structure has been kept as well as the beauty and meaning of these immortal poems. 121 Pages.

THE ROSE GARDEN OF MYSTERY: SHABISTARI
Translation by Paul Smith. Introduction by E.H. Whinfield & Paul Smith
The Rose Garden of Mystery was composed as a 1000 couplet long *masnavi* poem in the form of questions and answers on spiritual matters by Mahmud Shabistari of Tabriz in 1317 at the request of his Spiritual Master.
Since then it has been regarded as one of the finest books on Sufism.
E.G. Browne in his classic work, 'History of Persian Literature' calls this book "On the whole, one of the best manuals of Sufi theosophy that exists." Rev. John A. Subhan in his 'Sufism, Its Saints and Shrines' states, "We know little about the life of the author... But his work is important out of all comparison with the importance of the author because it is a compendium of

Sufi terminology in the form of question and answer."
The correct rhyme-structure has been kept in this complete, modern
translation, as well as the beauty and meaning of this beautiful, mystical,
poem. Selected Bibliography. Pages 182

RUDAKI: SELECTED POEMS
Translation, Introduction & Notes by Paul Smith
Abu 'Abd Allah Ja'far ibn Muhammad Rudaki (858-941) the 'father of
Persian Poetry' and possibly the *ruba'i,* was born in the village of Rudak
near Samarkand. First a wandering 'dervish' poet/minstrel he later served at
the court of the Samanids of Bokhara. Nasr ibn Ahmad summoned him to
his court and he prospered there amassing great wealth. He had 200 slaves
in his retinue... and 400 camels carried his belongings when he travelled.
In 937 he fell out of favour at court (and was blinded at this time as some
commentators suggest) after the death of the prime-minister who had
supported him. His life ended in abject poverty, forgotten by the world at
that time, perhaps the reason why so much of his vast output of 1,300,000
couplets, only 75 *rubai's, ghazals, qasidas* and *qit'as survive* (most are here
translated, the most published). Rudaki's poetry is about the passage of
time, old age, death, fortune's fickleness, importance of the matters of the
heart, the need to be happy. Although he praised kings, nobles and heroes...
his greatest love was knowledge and experience. The Introduction contains:
Persian Poetry, A New Beginning; The Life, Times and Poetry of Rudaki;
The Various Forms in the Poetry of Rudaki and a Selected Bibliography.
The correct rhyme-structure has been kept in this modern translation, as
well as the beauty and meaning of these beautiful poems. 140 pages.

SADI: SELECTED POEMS
Translation, Introduction & Notes by Paul Smith
Sadi of Shiraz, along with Hafiz, Nizami & Rumi is considered one of the
great mystical and romantic poets of Iran. His masterpieces, *The Rose
Garden* and *The Bustan* (Orchard) have been a major influence in the East
and West for the past 700 years. His *Divan* of *ghazals* are still much loved
by Iranians. His *ruba'is* have also been an influence on the poets that
followed him. Here is a large selection of his *ghazals, ruba'is* and *masnavis.*
Included is a long Introduction on his Life and Times and Poetry. There is
also a Selected Bibliography and Glossary of Sufi Symbols. The correct
rhyme-structure has been kept in this modern translation, as well as the
beauty and meaning of these beautiful poems. 207 pages.

JAMI: SELECTED POEMS
Translation, Introduction by Paul Smith
Jami (1414-1493), is still considered the last great poet of the Classical Period (10th-15th C.) of Persian Poetry is mostly known for his masterpiece seven *masnavi* epics... including his masterpieces Joseph and Zulaikh... also Layla and Majnun, Chain of Gold and Book of the Wisdom of Alexander. He also composed three *Divans* consisting of *ghazals rubai's* and other profound, mystical poems. Here is the largest number of his *ghazals* and *ruba'is* translated into English and a good selection from most of his *masnavis*. Included in the Introduction... the life of Jami and a chapter of Sufism in Persian Poetry and a chapter on the various forms of poetry he used and a Selected Bibliography. The correct rhyme-structure is kept as well as the beauty and meaning of these beautiful, mystical poems. 164 Pages.

NIZAMI: SELECTED POEMS
Translation & Introduction by Paul Smith
Nizami (d. 1208) is a true Sufi Master Poet who is most famous for his six books in *masnavi* form: *The Treasury of the Mysteries, Layla and Majnun, Khrosrau and Shirin, The Seven Portraits* and his two books on Alexander. He also composed a *Divan* of approximately 20,000 couplets mostly in *ghazals* and *ruba'is*... tragically only 200 couplets survive. His influence on Attar, Rumi, Sadi, Hafiz and Jami and all others that followed was profound. Here is the largest number of his *ghazals* and *ruba'is* and *qasidas* translated into English and a good selection from his *masnavis*. Included in the Introduction... the life and Times and Poetry of Nizami and on the various forms of poetry he used and a Selected Bibliography. The correct rhyme-structure has been kept as well as the beauty and meaning of these beautiful, mystical poems. 235 pages.

RUBA'IYAT OF BEDIL
Translation & Introduction by Paul Smith
Mirza Abdul-Qader Bedil (1644-1721) is one of the most respected poets originally from Afghanistan. In the early 17th century, his family moved from Balkh to India, to live under the Mughul dynasty. He was born and educated near Patna. In his later life he spent time travelling and visiting ancestral lands. His writings in Persian are extensive, being one of the creators of the 'Indian style'. He had complicated views on the nature of God, heavily influenced by the Sufis. Bedil's 16 books of poetry contain nearly 147,000 couplets with over 3600 poems that are *ruba'is*. He is now

considered a great later master of this form. The correct rhyme-structure is kept as well as the beauty and meaning of these beautiful, often mystical poems. 134 pages.

BEDIL: SELECTED POEMS
Translation & Introduction by Paul Smith
Mirza Abdul-Qader Bedil (1644-1721) is one of the most respected poets from Afghanistan. In the early 17th century, his family moved from Balkh to India, to live under the Mughul dynasty. He was born and educated near Patna. In his later life he spent time travelling and visiting ancestral lands. His writings in Persian are extensive, being one of the creators of the 'Indian style'. Bedil's 16 books of poetry contain nearly 147,000 couplets. With Ghalib he is considered a master of the complicated 'Indian Style' of the *ghazal*. He had complicated views on the nature of God, heavily influenced by the Sufis. The correct rhyme-structure has been kept as well as the beauty and meaning of these beautiful and often mystical poems. Pages... 144

ANVARI: SELECTED POEMS
Translation & Introduction by Paul Smith
Ahad-ud-din Anvari Abeverdi (1126-1189) was a court poet of the Seljuk sultans. Jami composed a *ruba'i* where he names him, along with Firdausi and Sadi as one of the 'three apostles' of Persian poetry. He was also a celebrated astronomer, mathematician and scientist who admitted he gave them up for the more lucrative occupation of ... a court poet, that he later rejected twenty years before his death for a life of seclusion and contemplation. He is renowned for his delightful wittiness that can be found in many of his *ruba'is* and *qit'as and ghazals*. He is one of the greatest Persian masters of the *qasida* and his one called 'The Tears of Khurasan' is considered his masterpieces. He is known for his sense of humour and sometimes obscenity. He created a new kind of poetry by using the conversational language of his time in simple words and expressions. The correct rhyme-structure has been kept as well as the beauty and meaning of these beautiful, poems. 156 pages.

RUBA'IYAT OF 'IRAQI
Translation & Introduction by Paul Smith
'Iraqi (1213-1289) was the author of a *Divan* of spiritual *ghazals* and *ruba'is* and the famous work in prose and poetry... *Lama'at*, 'Divine Flashes'... a classic of Sufi Mysticism. He was born in Hamadan in western Persia and as a child learnt the *Koran* by heart. He travelled from Persia to India with

dervishes where he stayed for 25 years. It is said that on his travels he met Rumi. His grave is in Damascus beside that of another great Perfect Master and poet Ibn al-'Arabi. When seeing these graves a pilgrim stated, "That ('Iraqi) is the Persian Gulf and this (Ibn al- 'Arabi) is the Arabian Sea." The correct rhyme-structure has been kept as well as the beauty and meaning of these beautiful, mystical poems. 116 pages.

THE WISDOM OF IBN YAMIN: SELECTED POEMS
Translation & Introduction Paul Smith
Amir Fakhr al-Din Mahmud, or Ibn Yamin (1286-1367), was born in Turkistan. His father was a poet who taught him the craft and left his son wealthy and the role of the court-poet in Khurasan. Ibn Yamin was taken captive when war broke out in 1342 and his complete *Divan* of poems was destroyed. He was a master of the form of the *qi'ta*. He is now as he was then, famous for his down-to-earth wisdom. Hafiz was probably influenced by his poems. During the last 25 years of his life he composed a further 5000 couplets on top of those he remembered. Here is the largest translation of his poems published in correct-rhyming, meaningful English. Introduction: Life & Times & Poetry, Forms in which he wrote, Bibliography. 155 pages.

NESIMI: SELECTED POEMS
Translation & Introduction by Paul Smith
Nesimi (1369-1417) is considered one of the greatest mystical poets of the late 14th and early 15th centuries and one of the most prominent early masters in Turkish/Azerbaijani literary history. For Nesimi at the centre of Creation there was God, who bestowed His Light on man. Through sacrifice and self-perfection, man can become one with Him. As a direct result of his beliefs he was skinned alive. His tomb in Aleppo remains an important place of pilgrimage to this day. His work consists of two collections of poems, one in Persian and the most important in Turkish that consists of 250-300 *ghazels* and about 175 *roba'is*. After his death his work continued to exercise an influence on Turkish language poets and authors. The 600th anniversary of Nesimi's birth was celebrated worldwide by UNESCO. The Introduction is on his Life & Times & Poetry and the Forms in which he wrote. The correct rhyme-structure has been kept as well as the beauty and meaning of these beautiful, mystical poems. 210 pages

ROBA'IYAT OF NESIMI
Translation & Introduction by Paul Smith
Nesimi (1369-1417) is one of the great spiritual poets of the late 14th and early 15th centuries and one of the masters in Turkish/Azerbaijani literary

history. For Nesimi at the centre of Creation there was God, who bestowed His Light on man. Through sacrifice and self-perfection, man can become one with Him. His poems were considered heresy and he skinned alive as punishment. His tomb in Aleppo remains an important place of pilgrimage to this day. His Turkish *roba'iyat* consists of about 175 *roba'is*, 13 in Persian (most are here translated). The 600th anniversary of Nesimi's birth was celebrated by UNESCO. The correct rhyme-structure has been kept as well as the beauty and meaning of these beautiful, mystical poems. 145 pages

SHAH NI'MATULLAH: SELECTED POEMS
Translation & Introduction by Paul Smith

Shah Ni'matullah Vali (1330-1431) was the founder of an order of Sufis that is today the largest in Iran. As well as a Sufi Master he was a poet who at times used 'Sayyid' as his *takhallus* or pen-name. He was influenced by Ibn 'Arabi and Hafiz. He came from Aleppo and after studies travelled in Egypt, Morocco, Mecca (where he met his Spiritual Master Abdullah Yafi'i). He built a monastery in Mahan near Kirman and lived there until his death. He composed many prose works on Sufism and his *Divan* contains over 13,000 couplets, mostly *ghazals* and *ruba'is*. This is the largest selection of his poems published in English. Introduction is on his Life & Times & Poetry and the Forms in which he wrote and on Sufism & Poetry. The correct rhyme-structure has been kept as well as the meaning of these beautiful, enlightened poems. Glossary, bibliography. 168 pages

AMIR KHUSRAU: SELECTED POEMS
Translation & Introduction by Paul Smith

Amir Khusrau (1253-1324), the 'Parrot of India' was born at Patigali near the Ganges in India. At the age of thirty-six he was poet-laureate, serving many sultans. He was not only fluent in Persian, in which he composed the majority of his 92 books, but also in Arabic, Hindi and Sanskrit. He composed ten long *masnavis*, five *Divans* of *ghazals* and other poems and many prose works. He was a Master musician and invented the *sitar*. The Perfect Master Nizam ud-din took him as his disciple and eventually he became God-realized. He rebelled against narrow spirituality and helped redefine the true Sufi way. He was a profound influence on Hafiz and is seen as the link between Sadi and Hafiz in updating the form and content of the *ghazal* and eroticising it. This is the largest selection of his poems in English. Introduction is on his Life & Times & Poetry and the Forms in which he wrote and on Sufism & Poetry. The correct rhyme-structure has been kept and the meaning of these beautiful, enlightened poems. 201 pages

A WEALTH OF POETS: Persian Poetry at the Courts of Sultan Mahmud in Ghazneh & Sultan Sanjar in Ganjeh (998-1158)
Translations, Introduction and Notes by Paul Smith
CONTENTS: Persian Poetry: A New Beginning... 7, Sultan Mahmud: His Life, Times and Poets 9. Sultan Sanjar: His Life, Times & Poets... 17. The Various Forms in Persian Poetry... 22, Sufism in Persian Poetry... 31. THE POETS: Poets at the Court of Sultan Mahmud... page 35, Sultan Mahmud 37, Umarah 39, Kisa'i 41, Firdausi 44, Farrukhi 55, Asjadi 67, Manuchirhri 69, Poet-laureate Unsuri 75, Asadi 82. Poets at the Court of Sultan Sanjar... page 89, Poet-laureate Mu'izzi 91, Sabir 101, Mahsati 105, Jabali 116, Vatvat 120, Anvari 124. The correct rhyme-structures have been kept and the meaning of these often beautiful, challenging, powerful and sometimes mystical poems. 158 pages

SHIMMERING JEWELS: Anthology of Poetry Under the Reigns of the Mughal Emperors of India (1526-1857)
Translations, Introductions, Etc. by Paul Smith
CONTENTS: The Mughal Empire... Page 7, Emperor Babur... 14, Emperor Humayun... 19, Emperor Akbar... 31, Emperor Jahangir... 44, Emperor Shah Jahan... 50, Emperor Aurangzeb... 57, Emperor Bahadur Shah Zafar... 71. Sufis & Dervishes: Their Art and Use of Poetry... 78, The Main Forms in Persian, Urdu & Pushtu Poetry of the Indian Sub-Continent... 81 Poets in the Reign of Babur... 91, Babur 93, Wafa'i 96, Farighi 97, Haqiri 98. Poets in the Reign of Humayun... 99, Humayun 102, Kamran 104, Nadiri 106, Bayram 107. Poets in the Reign of Akbar... 109, Akbar 111, Ghazali 113, Maili 116, Kahi 117, Faizi 119, Urfi 122, Nami 127, Hayati 130, Qutub Shah 132, Naziri 135. Poets in the Reign of Jahangir... 137, Jahangir 139, Rahim 140, Talib 142, Shikebi 160, Tausani 161, Qasim 162. Poets in the Reign of Shah Jahan... 163, Qudsi 165, Sa'ib 168, Kalim 172. Poets in Reign of Aurangzeb... 177, Dara Shikoh 179, Mullah Shah 186, Sarmad 189, Khushal 199, Nasir Ali 213, Makhfi 215, Wali 239, Bedil 243. Poets in the Reign of Bahadur Shah Zafar... 251, Zafar 253, Zauq 260, Ghalib 266, Momin 275, Shefta 280, Dagh 283. The correct rhyme-structures have been kept and the meaning of these often beautiful, powerful and sometimes mystical poems. Pages 292.

RAHMAN BABA: SELECTED POEMS
Translation & Introduction by Paul Smith
Rahman Baba (1652 to 1711) is considered the greatest Sufi Pashtun poet to compose poems, mainly *ghazals*, in the Pushtu language. Born in Mohmand

region of Afghanistan near Peshawar he was called 'The Nightingale of Peshawar'. This was a time of struggle and hardship and in the midst of the turmoil he was an excellent student with a natural gift for poetry.
He eventually questioned the value of such pursuits and withdrew from the world, dedicating himself to prayer and devotion. In solitary worship he began to write again and his poetry spread. Religious figures used it to inspire the devout, political leaders to inspire the independence movement. His *Divan* is 343 poems... *ghazals* and a few *qasidas* and *mukhammas*. Introduction is on his Life & Times & Poetry and the Forms in which he wrote and on Sufism & Poetry. The correct rhyme-structure is kept as well as the meaning of these beautiful, enlightened poems. 139 pages

RUBA'IYAT OF DARA SHIKOH
Translation & Introduction by Paul Smith
Dara Shikoh (1615-1659) was the oldest son of Emperor Shah Jahan and was known to be a loving husband , a good son and loving father. He was a fine poet, his poems having the influence of Sufism to which he was dedicated. He used 'Qadiri' as his *takhallus* or pen-name. His *Divan* of *ghazals, ruba'is* and *qasidas* in Persian was not the only work he left behind, his five prose works on Sufism and mysticism are popular in India even today. His *Majma al-Bahrain* or *The Mingling of the Two Oceans* is an explanation of the mystical sameness of Sufism and Vedanta. He also translated the *Upanishads, Bhagavad Gita* and *Yoga-Vasishta* into Persian. After he was defeated after leading an uprising against his cruel, fundamentalist brother Emperor Aurangzeb and was brutally killed in 1659. The correct rhyme-structure has been kept and the meaning of these beautiful, powerful mystical poems. This is the largest translation of his poems into English. 120 pages

ANTHOLOGY OF POETRY OF THE CHISHTI SUFI ORDER
Translations & Introduction by Paul Smith
The Chishti Order is a Sufi order within the mystic branches of Islam which was founded in Chisht, a small town near Herat, Afghanistan about 930 A.D. The Chishti Order is known for its emphasis on love, tolerance, and openness. The Master & Perfect Master Poets: Mu'in ud-din Chishti, Baba Farid, Nizam –ud-din Auliya, Amir Khusrau, Dara Shikoh, Inayat Khan, Khadim & others. Introduction on the Chishti Order of Sufism and the Spiritual forms of the Master Poets of this famous Order of the Indian Sub-Continent. The correct rhyme-structures have been kept and the meaning of these often beautiful, powerful and always spiritual poems. Pages 300.

RUBA'IYAT OF ANSARI
Translation & Introduction by Paul Smith

One of the greatest mystical poets and Perfect Masters of all time, Abdullah Ansari... who passed from this world 1089 in Herat was most famous for his biographical dictionary on saints and Sufi masters and his much loved collection of inspiring prayers, the *Munajat* among many works in Persian and Arabic. His *ruba'is* appear throughout his works. The correct rhyme-structure has been kept and the meaning of these beautiful, powerful, mystical poems. This is the largest translation of his *ruba'is* into English. 183 pages

RUBA'IYAT OF SHAH NI'MATULLAH
Translation & Introduction by Paul Smith

Shah Ni'matullah Vali (1330-1431) was the founder of an order of Sufis that is today the largest in Iran. As well as a Sufi Master he was a poet who at times used 'Sayyid' as his *takhallus* or pen-name. He was influenced by Ibn 'Arabi and Hafiz. He came from Aleppo and after studies travelled in Egypt, Morocco, Mecca (where he met his Spiritual Master Abdullah Yafi'i). He built a monastery in Mahan near Kirman and lived there until his death. He composed many prose works on Sufism and his *Divan* contains over 13,000 couplets, mostly *ghazals* and *ruba'is*. This is the largest selection of his *ruba'is* published in English. Introduction is on his Life & Times & Poetry and the meaning of Sufi poetry and a History of the Form and Function of the *Ruba'i*. The correct rhyme-structure has been kept as well as the meaning of these beautiful, enlightened poems. Glossary, bibliography. 125 pages

ANSARI: SELECTED POEMS
Translation & Introduction by Paul Smith

One of the greatest mystical poets and Perfect Masters of all time, Abdullah Ansari... who passed from this world 1089 in Herat was most famous for his biographical dictionary on saints and Sufi masters and his much loved collection of inspiring prayers, the *Munajat* among many works in Persian and Arabic. His *ruba'is* appear throughout his works and he composed three *Divans* in which his *ghazals* are in the majority. Here is a fine selection of them and a *qasida*. The correct rhyme-structure has been kept and the meaning of these beautiful, powerful, mystical poems. This is the largest translation of his poems into English. 156 pages

BABA FARID: SELECTED POEMS
Translation & Introduction by Paul Smith
The father of Punjabi poetry Baba Farid (1173-1266) was born in the Punjab.
Khwaja Bakhtiar Kaki was Baba Farid's Spiritual Master. Kaki met Mu'in
ud-din Chishti at Baghdad and became his disciple. The king at Delhi,
Balban, welcomed Farid in Delhi. His daughter married Farid. Baba Farid,
the Sufi Master poet laureate from Punjab is famous for his wise and
spiritual couplets (slokas)... 112 of them are in the bible of the Sikhs (whom
he influenced) the Guru Granth, and 128 are translated here with the correct
rhyme-structure and meaning. Hospitals and factories and even a town
named after him. 164 pages.

POETS OF THE NI'MATULLAH SUFI ORDER
Translations & Introduction by Paul Smith
Shah Ni'matullah (1330-1431) was the founder of an order of Sufis that is
today one of the largest in Iran and around the world. As well as a Sufi
Master he was a poet who inspired many Spiritual Masters and Sufi Poets
over the following 500 years to follow his example.
CONTENTS: The Ni'matullah Sufi Order... page 7, Sufis & Dervishes:
Their Art & Use of Poetry... 10, Forms of Poetry used by the Ni'matullah
Poets... 26, Selected Bibliography... 35, Glossary... 36
The Poets...Shah Ni'matullah... 39, Bushaq... 85, Kasim Anwar... 117,
Shah Da'i... 145, Nur 'Ali Shah... 167, Bibi Hayati... 178, Rida 'Ali Shah...
209, Muzaffar 'Ali Shah... 221, Khusrawi... 230, Munis 'Ali Shah... 236.
The correct rhyme-structures have been kept and the meaning of these
beautiful, powerful and mystical poems. This is the largest translation of
their poems into English. 244 pages.

MU'IN UD-DIN CHISHTI: SELECTED POEMS
Translation & Introduction by Paul Smith
Mu'in ud-din Chishti (1141-1230) was also known as Gharib Nawaz or
'Benefactor of the Poor', he is the most famous Sufi saint of the Chishti
Order of the Indian Subcontinent. He also composed many ghazals . In his
book Pre Mughal Persian in Hindustan, Muhammad 'Abdu'l Ghani
states... "He was the greatest lyric poet of his age. His style is exuberant
and precise at once. His poems are a storehouse of transcendental thoughts
beautifully ordered and forcefully expressed. There is always a sense of
pious serenity and joy in his verses which are teeming with Divine Love...
his poetry resembles closely that of Hafiz... He takes his readers along
with him solely to spiritual ecstasy and gives them a peep into the ethereal

world..." Today, hundreds of thousands of people... Muslims, Hindus, Christians and others take grace from his tomb and poems. This is the largest selection of his *ghazals* translated into English in the correct form and meaning. 171 pages.

QASIDAH BURDAH:
THE THREE POEMS OF THE PROPHET'S MANTLE
Translations & Introduction by Paul Smith

Ka'b ibn Zuhair (died 7th century A.D.) was a famous poet who at first opposed Prophet Muhammad. Finally, he secretly went to Medina and approached the Prophet to ask if one who repented and embraced the faith would be forgiven. Mohammed answered yes and the poet asked, "Even Ka'b ibn Zuhair?" When he affirmed this, Ka'b revealed his identity and read a poem, his *Banat Suad* (of 55 couplets), which would become his most famous poem. As a reward Prophet Mohammed took off his mantle (cloak) and put it on Ka'b's shoulders. The second 'Mantle' *qasida* (ode) of praise for Mohammed was composed by the eminent Sufi, Imam al-Busiri (1210-1297). The poem (161 couplets) is famous mainly in the Sunni Muslim world. It is entirely in praise of Prophet Mohammed, who is said to have cured the poet of paralysis by appearing to him in a dream and wrapping him in a mantle. The third poet of the 'Mantle' was Ahmed Shawqi (1869 - 1932) the great Arabic Poet-Laureate, an Egyptian poet and dramatist who pioneered the modern Egyptian literary movement, most notably introducing the genre of poetic epics to the Arabic literary tradition. His 'Mantle' *qasida* is 190 couplets. The correct rhyme-structure has been kept and the meaning of these beautiful, powerful, spiritual poems. Pages 116

KHUSHAL KHAN KHATTAK: THE GREAT POET & WARRIOR OF AFGHANISTAN, SELECTED POEMS
Translation & Introduction by Paul Smith

Khushal Khan Khattak (1613-1689) was a Pashtun poet, warrior, and chief of the Khattak tribe. He wrote in Pashtu during the reign of the Mughals and fought the fanatic Aurangzeb and admonished Afghans to forsake their divisive tendencies and unite. He was the father of fifty-seven sons, some of them fine poets and thirty daughters. He is the author of over 200 works in Pushtu and Persian, consisting of Poetry, Medicine, Ethics, Religious Jurisprudence, Philosophy, Falconry, etc., together with an account of the events of his own life. His poetry is said to consist of more than 45,000 poems! There is not another poet in the Afghan language of Pashtu who created so many poems on such a wide range of subjects. He wrote *ghazals*, *ruba'is*, *qasidas*, *qi'tas* and *masnavis*. Introduction on his life, times &

poetry. The correct rhyme-structure has been kept and the meaning of these beautiful, powerful, and occasionally spiritual poems. Pages 187

'IRAQI: SELECTED POEMS
Translation & Introduction by Paul Smith
'Iraqi (1213-1289) was the author of a *Divan* of spiritual *ghazals* and *ruba'is* and the famous work in prose and poetry... *Lama'at*, 'Divine Flashes'... a classic of Sufi Mysticism. He was born in Hamadan in western Persia and as a child learnt the *Koran* by heart. He travelled from Persia to India with dervishes where he stayed for 25 years. It is said that on his travels he met Rumi. His grave is in Damascus beside that of another great Perfect Master and poet Ibn al-'Arabi. When seeing these graves a pilgrim stated, "That ('Iraqi) is the Persian Gulf and this (Ibn al- 'Arabi) is the Arabian Sea." Introduction: The Life & Times & Poems of 'Iraqi, Selected Bibliography, Forms in Classical Persian Poetry Used by 'Iraqi. *Rubai's, Ghazals, Qasida, Masnavis, Tarji-band*. The correct rhyme-structure has been kept as well as the beauty and meaning of these beautiful, mystical poems. 158 pages.

MANSUR HALLAJ: SELECTED POEMS
Translation & Introduction by Paul Smith
The Perfect Master, poet & martyr, Husayn Mansur al-Hallaj (died 919), was born in Shiraz and tortured and executed in Baghdad for declaring: "I am the Truth *(Anal Haq)."* Much has been written about his famous (and infamous) statement, but few of his powerful, often mysteries and always deeply conscious and spiritual poems in Arabic have been translated before from his *Divan* into English, and in the poetic form in which they were composed. The Introduction contains: The Life, Times and Works of Mansur Hallaj, The Perfect Master *(Qutub)*, 'Anal-Haq' or 'I am the Truth' of Mansur Hallaj, Four Master Poets of Baghdad who influenced Hallaj, Sufis & Dervishes: Their Art & Use of Poetry. There is a wide selection of his *qit'as, ghazals, ruba'is, qasidas*. Included are two appendixes: A Selection of Poetry from the Persian, Turkish & Pashtu poetry about or influenced by him, and the *Tawasin* of Mansur al-Hallaj. Translated by Aish Abd Ar-Rahman At-Tarjumana. Pages 209.

RUBA'IYAT OF BABA AFZAL
Translation & Introduction by Paul Smith
Baba Afzal (1186-1256) came from Maraq near Kashan. He is the author of many Persian works on philosophical and metaphysical subjects and translated the Arabic version of Aristotle's 'The Book of the Soul' into

Persian. He was a Sufi and the author of about 500 mystical and at times controversial *ruba'is* some that have been mistakenly identified as Khayyam's. Some of the themes in these include warnings about the futility of involvement with the things of the world, correspondence between microcosm and macrocosm and self-knowledge as the goal of human existence. He is one of the greatest poets among the philosophers of Islam. Introduction includes: The Life, Times & Work of Baba Afzal, Sufis: Their Art & Use of Poetry, The *Ruba'i:* Its Form, Use & History. The correct rhyme-structure has been kept as well as the beauty and meaning of these poems. 178 pages.

RUMI: SELECTIONS FROM HIS *MASNAVI*
Translation & Introduction by Paul Smith
The *masnavi* is the form used in Persian and other languages to write epic ballads or romances and it is essentially a Persian invention. The most famous poems written in this form are the 'Shahnama' (Book of the Kings) of Firdausi, the 'Enclosed Garden of the Truth' of Sana'i, the 'Five Treasures' of Nizami, the 'Conference of the Birds' and 'The Book of God' and many others by 'Attar, the 'Seven Thrones' of Jami, the ten *masnavis* of Amir Khusrau and of course the greatest of them all… the 'Masnavi' of Rumi. Many *masnavis* by the great Perfect Master Poets were of a Sufi/Dervish mystical nature. Included in this volume is a chapter on The Life, Times & Poetry of Rumi and one on the history of the *masnavi* in Persian poetry by the various masters in this form with translations of their works up until Rumi. From Rumi's *Masnavi* are his Introduction to the 6 volumes and the first three Tales in full and excerpts from the whole work, including some of his ribald tales. Selected Bibliography. The correct rhyme-form of the *masnavi* has been kept in all the translations. 260 pages.

THE WINE OF LOVE: AN ANTHOLOGY,
Wine in the Poetry of Arabia, Persia, Turkey & the Indian Sub-Continent from Pre-Islamic Times to the Present
Translations & Introduction by Paul Smith
CONTENTS Arabic Poetry 7, Persian Poetry 11, Turkish Poetry 13, Pushtu Poetry 15, Urdu Poetry 17, The Main Forms in Arabic, Persian, Turkish, Pushtu & Urdu Poetry 19, Wine in Sufi Poetry 29, Arabic Poetry… 37, Ima'-ul-Qays 39, Antara 47, Tarafa 59, Amru 72, Labid 80, Ka'b 92, Omar Ibn abi Rabi'a 96, Majnun 98, Rabi'a of Basra 101, Abu Nuwas 106, Bayazid Bastami 114, Al-Mutanabbi 116, Al-Ma'arri 131, Gilani 134, Suhrawadi 137, Ibn al-Farid 140, Ibn 'Arabi 145, Al-Shushtari 148. Persian Poetry… 151, Abu Shakur 153, Junaidi 155, Rudaki 157, Agachi

172, Rabi'a Balkhi 174, Daqiqi 177, Umarah 181, Kisa'i 183, Farrukhi 185, Asjadi 193, Minuchihri 195, Unsuri 198, Abu Sa'id 201, Baba Kuhi 203, Qatran 205, Ansari 207, Al-Ghazali 212, Mas'ud Sa'd 214, Mu'izzi 216, Omar Khayyam 219, Sana'l 227, Sabir 232, Mahsati 235, Jabali 238, Vatvat 240, Anvari 242, Falaki 246, Hasan Ghaznavi 249, Athir 252, Mujir 255, Khaqani 257, Mu'in 266, Zahir 274, Nizami 278, Ruzbihan 284, 'Attar 286, Auhad ud-din Kermani 292, Kamal ad-din 294, Baba Afzal 297, Rumi 299, Sadi 310, 'Iraqi 323, Humam 335, Amir Khusray 337, Hasan Dihlavi 347, Khaju 351, Obeyd Zakani 353, Emad 361, Salman 366, Shahin 371, Hafiz 374, Ruh Attar 396, Haydar 401, Junaid Shirazi 404, Jahan Khatun 406, Maghribi 413, Bushaq 415, Kasim Anwar 419, Shah Ni'matu'llah 422, Jami 425, Ahli 428, Helali 430, Fighani 432, Babur 435, Ghazali 437, Urfi 439, Lotfali Suratgar 493, Rahi 495. Turkish Poetry... 497, Ahmed Yesevi 499, Yunus Emre 502, Kadi Burhan-ud-din 507, Nesimi 509, Mihri 515, Necati 518, Pir Sultan 523, Khayali 535, Fuzuli 528, Baqi 535, Huda'l 539, Nef'l 541, Yahya 544, Na'ila 546, Nabi 548, Nedim 550, Fitnet 553, Galib 555, Leyla Khanim 562. Pushtu Poetry... 565, Mirza 567, Khushal 570, Ashraf Khan 578, Abdul-Khadir 580, Rahman Baba 585, Khwaja Mohammad 588, Shaida 592. Urdu Poetry... 595, Wali 587, Sauda 599, Dard 601, Nazir 603, Mir 606, Zauq 610, Ghalib 612, Momin 619, Dagh 621, Shad 623, Iqbal 625, Ashgar 629, Josh 631, Jigar 633, Huma 637, Firaq 641, Faiz 643. 645 pages.

GHALIB: SELECTED POEMS
Translation & Introduction by Paul Smith
Mirza Asadullah Beg (1797-1869), known as Ghalib (conqueror), was born in the city of Agra of parents with Turkish aristocratic ancestry. When he was only five his father Abdullah Beg Khan died in a battle while working under Rao Raja Bakhtwar. Ghalib's fame came to him posthumously. He had himself remarked during his lifetime that although his age had ignored his greatness, it would be recognised by later generations. History has vindicated his claim. Ghalib wrote beautiful *ghazals* and other poems in Persian... over 250 (many are translated here) but is more famous for his *ghazals* written in Urdu. Before Ghalib, the Urdu *ghazal* was primarily an expression of anguished love, but Ghalib expressed his philosophy and cynicism on God and other subjects. His Urdu *Divan* contains 263 *ghazals* and a small number of *ruba'is, masnavis, qasidas* and *qit'as*. There have been many movies based on his life made in India and Pakistan where his popularity has never flagged. Introduction on his Life, Poetry and Times and the Forms of Poetry he wrote in. The correct rhyme-structure has been kept as well as the beauty and meaning of these poems. Pages 200.

THE ENLIGHTENED SAYINGS OF HAZRAT 'ALI
The Right Hand of the Prophet
Translation & Introduction by Paul Smith
Hazrat 'Ali (598-661) was Prophet Mohammed's nephew, son-in-law and favourite and was the first Imam of the Shi'ites and the fourth of the true caliphs of the Sunnis. Sufi Masters believe in Ali as one of the 'Seven Great Ones' in the first generation of teachers and many in orders of Dervishes trace their spiritual ancestry back to him. Hazrat Ali's sayings are published as *Nahj al-Balagh* or 'The Peak of Experience'... a treasury of wisdom and divine grace. It is said that he wrote the original *Koran* in his own blood as Prophet Mohammed gave it. He also composed a *Divan* of enlightened poetry and one of his important, profound *ghazals* is translated in the Introduction to this book. Pages 260.

HAFIZ: TONGUE OF THE HIDDEN
A Selection of *Ghazals* from his *Divan*
Translation & Introduction Paul Smith
This is the completely revised third edition of a selection of Hafiz's *ghazals* from his Divan his masterpiece of 791 *ghazals, masnavis, rubais* and other poems/songs. The spiritual and historical and human content is here in understandable, beautiful poetry: the correct rhyme-structure has been achieved, without intruding, in readable English. In the Introduction his life story is told in great detail; his spirituality is explored, the form and function of his poetry, Glossary, Selected Bibliography. 133 pages. Third Edition.

HAFIZ: THE SUN OF SHIRAZ
Essays, Talks, Projects on the Immortal Poet
Paul Smith
CONTENTS: Introduction by Richard Lee; The Life of Hafiz; Hafiz's Influence on the East & the West, The English Translations of Hafiz; Hafiz and His Translator, Sufism and God; Poetry, Life and Times of Hafiz of Shiraz; UNESCO and Hafiz; Hafiz for Our Time; Preface to Original Divan. 249 pages

~ HAFIZ: A DAYBOOK ~
Translation & Introduction by Paul Smith
Hafiz is considered by many of the world's foremost poets, mystics, artists and writers to be the greatest poet of all time. Hafiz was not only a great poet, he became a Perfect Master or enlightened being, whose wisdom and insights into the everyday and mystical path are such that it is said that one

can gain spiritual advancement by reading his book. During the past six centuries he has inspired and influenced the world of literature, philosophy, mysticism and all aspects of art: poetry, painting and music in the east and the west. His life was for mankind and his work to be shared with the world. Through his example we can learn how to prepare for unprecedented change. Without doubt, he is one of the greatest human beings since time began. His *Divan* has been loved by many millions of people. To this day it is used as an oracle and spiritual guide and in this Daybook one can use his couplets on a daily basis or open them at random for inspiration and advice. 375 pages.

~* RUMI* ~ A Daybook
Translation & Introduction by Paul Smith
The great Sufi Master and poet Jalal-ud-din Rumi was born in 1207 in Balkh. Rumi's love and his great longing for the Perfect Master Shams –e Tabriz found expression in music, dance, songs and poems in his collection of poems/songs or *Divan*. This vast work included thousands of *ghazals* and other poetic forms and nearly two thousand *ruba'is* which he would compose for many years, before he became a God-realised Perfect Master himself and also afterwards. Most of the poems in this Daybook are taken from his collection of *ruba'is,* but there are also selected couplets from his *ghazals* and his profound *Masnavi*. Introduction on his Life and Times, Selected Bibliography. The correct rhyme-structure has been kept in all 366 poems. Pages 383.

SUFI POETRY OF INDIA ~ A Daybook~
Translation & Introduction by Paul Smith
This is a Daybook of Sufi and Dervish Poetry of India in various poetic forms. Over 400 inspirational and spiritually helpful and beautiful poems to inspire and make your day. CONTENTS: The Poets, Sufis & Dervishes: Their Art and Use of Poetry, Glossary, The Main Forms in Persian, Punjabi, Hindi, Kashmiri, Sindhi and Urdu Sufi and Dervish Poetry of India, Selected Bibliography… THE POETS: Mu'in ud-din Chishti, Baba Farid, Amir Khusrau, Hasan Dihlavi, Lalla Ded, Kabir, Qutub Shah, Dara Shikoh, Sarmad, Sultan Bahu, Nasir Ali, Makhfi, Wali, Bedil, Bulleh Shah, Shah Latif, Ali Haider, Sauda, Dard, Nazir, Mir, Sachal Sarmast, Aatish, Zafar, Zauq, Ghalib, Dabir, Anees, Hali, Farid, Shad, Iqbal, Inayat Khan, Asghar, Jigar, Huma, Firaq, Josh. Pages 404.

~ SUFI POETRY~ A Daybook
Translation & Introduction by Paul Smith
This is a Daybook of Sufi and Dervish Poetry in the *Ruba'i* form, from the
Arabic, Persian, Turkish & Urdu from Rudaki to Modern Times. 366
inspirational and spiritually helpful and beautiful poems by the greatest
Sufi poets of all time including Rudaki, Mansur Hallaj, Shibli, Baba Tahir,
Abu Said, Ibn Sina, Baba Kuhi, Ansari, Al-Ghazali, Hamadani, Khayyam,
Sana'i, Mahsati, Khaqani, Nizami, Ruzbihan, Baghdadi, 'Attar, Auhad-
ud-din Kermani, Kamal ad-din, Hamavi, Baba Afzal, Rumi, Imami, Sadi,
'Iraqi, Humam, Amir Khusrau, Simnani, Ibn Yamin, Khaju, Obeyd
Zakani, Emad, Hafiz, Ruh Attar, Kadi Burhan-ud-din, Jahan Khatun,
Maghribi, Nesimi, Kasim Anwar, Shah Ni'matullah, Jami, Baba Fighani,
Fuzuli, Ghazali, Urfi, Qutub Shah, Haleti, Dara Shikoh, Sarmad, Sa'ib,
Makhfi, Bedil, Mushtaq, Sauda, Esrar Dede, Hatif, Mir, Aatish, Zauq,
Dabir, Anees, Hali, Shad, Iqbal, Khalili, Rahi, Firaq, Josh, Nurbakhsh,
Paul. Sufis & Dervishes, Their Art & Use of Poetry, The Form &
Function of the *Ruba'i*. Pages 390.

~*KABIR*~ A Daybook
Translation & Introduction by Paul Smith
'Here are wonderful words of wisdom (*sakhis*/poems) from one of the wisest
of the wise. Here are lines of love from a Master of Divine Love, and a
human being who has lived as all human beings should live, with
compassion, honesty and courage. If you want the Truth, no holds barred, it
is here, but as we're told; truth is dangerous! These poems change people.
You will not be the same! As Kabir says. "Wake up sleepy head!" ' From
the Introduction that includes a Glossary and a Selected Bibliography. 366
wonderful short poems in this Daybook to inspire and enlighten. 382 pages.

~ABU SA'ID & SARMAD~ A Sufi Daybook
Translation & Introduction by Paul Smith
Abu Sa'id (968-1049) was a Perfect Master and a poet who lived in
Nishapur and composed only *ruba'is*, over 400 of them. He was a founder of
Sufi poetry and a major influence on the *ruba'i* and most poets that
followed, especially Sana'i, Nizami, 'Attar, Rumi and Hafiz. Sarmad (d.
1659) was a famous and infamous Persian dervish poet of Jewish and
Armenian origin. As a merchant he gathered his wares and travelled to
India to sell them. In India he renounced Judaism and adopted Islam: he
later renounced it in favour of Hinduism which he finally renounced for
Sufism. He was known for exposing and ridiculing the major religions and
hypocrisy of his day, but he also wrote beautiful mystical poetry in the form

of *rubai's*. He was beheaded in 1659 by Emperor Aurangzeb for his perceived heretical poetry. This Sufi Daybook consists of 366 of their insightful, beautiful & spiritual *ruba'is*, 188 each. Introduction & Bibliography. 390 pages.

~*SADI*~ A Daybook
Translation & Introduction by Paul Smith
Sadi of Shiraz, along with Hafiz, Nizami & Rumi is considered one of the great mystical and romantic poets of Persia. His masterpieces, *The Rose Garden* and *The Bustan* (Orchard) have been a major influence in the East and West for the past 700 years. His *Divan* of *ghazals* are still much loved. His *ruba'is* have also been an influence on the poets that followed him. Here is a Daybook with a selection of 366 poems from his *ghazals*, *ruba'is* and *masnavis*. Introduction includes his Life and Times and Poetry. There is also a Selected Bibliography. The correct rhyme-structure has been kept as well as the beauty and meaning of these beautiful, inspirational and spiritual poems. A Daybook to remember each day. 394 pages.

NIZAMI, KHAYYAM & 'IRAQI ... A Daybook
Translation & Introduction by Paul Smith
Here is a unique Daybook of 366 poems by three of Persia's greatest mystical & philosophical poets. Nizami was a true Master Poet who is most famous for his six books in *masnavi* form: *The Treasury of the Mysteries, Khrosrau and Shirin, Layla and Majnun, The Seven Portraits* (another Sufi classic) and his two books on Alexander. He also composed a *Divan* of approximately 20,000 couplets in *ghazals* and *ruba'is* and other forms... tragically only 200 couplets survive. His influence on 'Attar, Rumi, Sadi, Hafiz and Jami and all others that followed cannot be overestimated. Omar Khayyam was more famous in Persia as an astronomer, philosopher and mathematician... the hedonistic and occasionally Sufi philosophy in his *ruba'is* meant that his poems were never really popular in his homeland, but of course after the work of FitzGerald the west fell in love with him. He stated, "The only group which may reach God with purification of soul and renunciation of sensual preoccupations, with yearning and ecstasy, are the Sufis." 'Iraqi was the author of a *Divan* of spiritual *ghazals* and *ruba'is* and other poems and of the famous work in prose and poetry *Lama'at*, 'Divine Flashes'... a work that beautifully describes the mysteries of Divine Union that became a classic of Sufi Mysticism. The correct rhyme structure has been kept. 380 pages.

~ABU SA'ID & SARMAD~ A Sufi Daybook
Translation & Introduction by Paul Smith
Abu Sa'id (968-1049) was a Perfect Master and a poet who lived in
Nishapur and composed only ruba'is, over 400 of them. He was a founder of
Sufi poetry and a major influence on the ruba'i and most poets that
followed, especially Sana'i, Nizami, 'Attar, Rumi and Hafiz. Sarmad (d.
1659) was a famous and infamous Persian dervish poet of Jewish and
Armenian origin. As a merchant he gathered his wares and travelled to
India to sell them. In India he renounced Judaism and adopted Islam: he
later renounced it in favour of Hinduism which he finally renounced for
Sufism. He was known for exposing and ridiculing the major religions and
hypocrisy of his day, but he also wrote beautiful mystical poetry in the form
of rubai's. He was beheaded in 1659 by Emperor Aurangzeb for his perceived
heretical poetry. This Sufi Daybook consists of 366 of their insightful,
beautiful & spiritual ruba'is, 188 each. Introduction & Bibliography. 390
pages.

ARABIC & AFGHAN SUFI POETRY ... A Daybook
Translation & Introduction by Paul Smith
Here is an enlightened Daybook of 366 inspirational poems by the greatest
Arabic & Afghan Sufi poets of all time in the forms of the ruba'i, ghazal
and others. THE POETS: ARABIC POETS: Hazrat Ali, Ali Ibn
Husain, Rabi'a of Basra, Abu Nuwas, Dhu'l-Nun, Bayazid Bistami, Al
Nuri, Junaid, Sumnun, Mansur al-Hallaj, Ibn 'Ata, Shibli, Ibn Sina, Al-
Ghazzali, Gilani, Abu Madyam, Suhrawadi, Ibn al-Farid, Ibn 'Arabi, Al-
Busiri, Al-Shushtari, Ahmed Shawqi. AFGHAN POETS: Mirza,
Khushal, Ashraf Khan, Bedil, Abdul-Kadir, Rahman Baba, Khwaja
Mohammad, Hamid, Ahmad Shah, Shaida, Khalili. The correct form and
meaning has been kept in all of these spiritual poems. Introduction on the
Spiritual meaning of Sufi poetry and its various forms. 392 pages.

TURKISH & URDU SUFI POETS... A Daybook
Translation & Introduction by Paul Smith
Here is an enlightened Daybook of 366 inspirational poems by the greatest
Turkish & Urdu Sufi poets of all time in the forms of the ruba'i, ghazal and
others. THE POETS: Turkish... Ahmed Yesevi, Sultan Valad, Yunus
Emre, Kadi Burhan-ud-din, Nesimi, Ahmedi, Suleyman Chelebi, Sheykhi,
Necati, Zati, Pir Sultan, Khayali, Fuzuli, Baqi, Huda'i, Nef'i, Yahya,
Haleti, Na'ili, Niyazi, Galib, Esrar Dede, Leyla Khanim, Veysel. Urdu...
Qutub Shah, Wali, Sauda, Dard, Nazir, Mir, Aatish, Zafar, Zauq,
Momin, Dabir, Anees, Hali, Shad, Inayat Khan, Iqbal, Asghar, Jigar. The

correct form and meaning has been kept in all of these spiritual poems. Introduction on Turkish, Urdu Poetry and the Spiritual meaning of Sufi poetry. 394 pages.

SUFI & DERVISH RUBA'IYAT (9th – 14th century) ~ A Daybook~
Translation & Introduction by Paul Smith
Here is an enlightened Daybook of 366 inspirational poems in the form of the *ruba'i* by the greatest Sufi & Dervish poets and Spiritual Masters from the 9th to the 14th century. THE POETS: Rudaki, Mansur al-Hallaj, Shibli, Baba Tahir, Abu Said, Ibn Sina, Baba Kuhi, Ansari, Al-Ghazali, Hamadani, Omar Khayyam, Sana'i, Mahsati, Khaqani, Nizami, Ruzbihan, Baghdadi, 'Attar, Auhad-ud-din Kermani, Kamal ad-din, Hamavi, Baba Afzal, Rumi, Imami, Sadi, 'Iraqi, Sultan Valad, Humam, Amir Khusrau, Simnani, Ibn Yamin, Khaju, Obeyd Zakani, Emad, Hafiz. Introduction is on Sufi Poetry and on the form & function of the *ruba'i*. 394 pages.

SUFI & DERVISH RUBA'IYAT (14thth – 20th century) ~ A Daybook~
Translation & Introduction by Paul Smith
Here is an enlightened Daybook of 366 inspirational poems in the form of the *ruba'i* by the greatest Sufi & Dervish poets and Spiritual Masters from the 14th to the 20th century. THE POETS: Hafiz, Ruh Attar, Kadi Burhan-ud-din, Jahan Khatun, Kamal, Maghribi, Nesimi, Kasim Anwar, Shah Ni'matullah, Jami, Baba Fighani, Fuzuli, Ghazali, Urfi, Qutub Shah, Haleti, Dara Shikoh, Sarmad, Sa'ib, Nasir Ali, Makhfi, Bedil, Mushtaq, Sauda, Dard, Esrar Dede, Hatif, Mir, Aatish, Zauq, Dabir, Anees, Hali, Shad, Iqbal, Mehroom, Khalili, Nurbakhsh, Paul. Introduction is on Sufi Poetry and on the form & function of the *ruba'i*. 394 pages.

ABU NUWAS Selected Poems
Translation & Introduction by Paul Smith
Abu Nuwas (757-814) was the most famous and infamous poet who composed in Arabic of the Abbasid era. His style was extravagant and his compositions reflected the licentious manners of the upper classes of his day. His father was Arab and his mother was Persian. As a youth he was sold into slavery; a wealthy benefactor later set him free. By the time he reached manhood he had settled in Baghdad and was composing poetry. It was at this time, because of his long hair, he acquired the name Abu Nuwas (Father of Ringlets). Gradually he attracted the attention of Harun al-Rashid and was given quarters at court. His ability as a poet no doubt was one reason for Abu Nuwas' success with the caliph, but after a while he

became known as a reprobate and participated in less reputable pastimes with the ruler. He spent time in Egypt but soon returned to Baghdad to live out his remaining years. It is said he lived the last part of his life as a Sufi and some of his poems reflect this. He is popular today, perhaps more so than he ever was, as a kind of comic anti-hero in many Muslim countries. His poems consist of qit'as (of which he was the first master) ghazals and qasidas. His poems could be classified into: praises (of nobles and caliphs & famous people), mockeries, jokes, complaints, love of men and women, wine, hunting, laments, asceticism. All forms are here in the true meaning & rhyme structure. Introduction on his Life, Times & Poetry and forms he composed in and an Appendix of some of the stories about him in the Arabian Nights. 154 pages.

~*NAZIR AKBARABADI*~ Selected Poems
Translation and Introduction Paul Smith
Nazir Akbarabadi (1735-1830) is an Indian poet known as the 'Father of Nazm', who wrote mainly Urdu ghazals and nazms. It is said that Nazir's poetic treasure consisted of about 200,000 but only about 6000 couplets remain. The canvas of Nazir's nazms is so vast that it encompasses all aspects of human behavior and every person can find nazms that can suit his taste. Many of his poems are about daily life and observations of things such as training a young bear or the pleasures of the rainy season, how beauty can fade, the lives of old prostitutes, etc. His poems are loved by folk today. Many of his poems are spiritual and he is seen as a true Sufi. Bankey Behari: 'He saw the Lord everywhere. His meditations led him to the realization of the Forms of the Lord as well as the Formless Divinity. He sings of Shri Krishna with the greatest fervour as of Hazrat Ali and the Prophet Mohammed, and turns his face if he comes across the pseudo-saints and religious preceptors who are wanting in realization and yet profess it. By far he is best in portraying the heat of his yearning for his vision.' This is the largest translation of his poetry into English, with the correct form & meaning. Introduction on his Life, Times & Poetry and on the poetic forms he used. Selected Bibliography. 191 pages.

GREAT SUFI POETS OF THE PUNJAB & SINDH: AN ANTHOLOGY
Translations, Introductions by Paul Smith
The ideal of the Punjabi & Sindhi Sufi poets was to find God in all His creation and thus attain union with Him. Thus union or annihilation in God was to be fully achieved after death, but in some cases it was gained while living. This Sufi poetry consequently is full of poems, songs, and

hymns praising the Beloved, describing the pain and sorrow inflicted by separation, and ultimately the joy, peace and knowledge attained in the union. CONTENTS: Introduction: Sufis & Dervishes: Their Art and Use of Poetry... 7, Sufi Poets of the Punjab... 33, Sufi Poets of Sindh...37 THE POETS... Baba Farid... 41, Sultan Bahu... 69, Bulleh Shah... 85, Ali Haider... 113, Farid... 123, Shah Latif... 133, Sachal Sarmast... 155. The correct rhyme-structure and spiritual meaning has been kept in these beautiful, spiritual & inspiring poems. 166 pages.

~RUBA'IYAT OF IQBAL~
Translation & Introduction by Paul Smith

Muhammad Iqbal (1873-1938) was born in Sialkot, Punjab. He graduated from Government College, Lahore with a master's degree in philosophy. He taught there while he established his reputation as an Urdu poet. During this period his poetry expressed an ardent Indian nationalism, but a marked change came over his views when he was studying for his doctorate at Cambridge, visiting German universities and qualifying as a barrister. The philosophies of Nietzsche and Bergson influenced him and he became critical of Western civilization that he regarded as decadent. He turned to Islam and Sufism for inspiration and rejected nationalism as a disease of the West. These ideas found expression in his long poems written in Persian, presumably to gain his ideas an audience in the Moslem world outside India. Becoming convinced that Muslims were in danger from the Hindu majority if India should become independent, he gave his support to Jinnah as the leader of India's Muslims. He is perhaps the last great master of the famous four-line *ruba'i* form of poetry, having composed over 550 of them in Persian & Urdu. Here is the largest collection of his *ruba'is* in English in book form, in the correct rhyme-structure and meaning. Introduction on his life, times & poetry and the form, function & history of the *ruba'i*. Bibliography. 175 pages.

~*IQBAL*~ SELECTED POETRY
Translation & Introduction by Paul Smith

Muhammad Iqbal (1873-1938) was born in Sialkot, Punjab. He graduated from Government College, Lahore with a master's degree in philosophy. He taught there while he established his reputation as an Urdu poet. During this period his poetry expressed an ardent Indian nationalism, but a marked change came over his views when he was studying for his doctorate at Cambridge, visiting German universities and qualifying as a barrister. The philosophies of Nietzsche and Bergson influenced him and he became critical of Western civilization that he regarded as decadent. He turned to

Islam and Sufism for inspiration and rejected nationalism as a disease of the West. These ideas found expression in his long poems written in Persian, presumably to gain his ideas an audience in the Moslem world outside India. Becoming convinced that Muslims were in danger from the Hindu majority if India should become independent, he gave his support to Jinnah as the leader of India's Muslims. In his final years he returned to Urdu as his medium with *ghazals* inspired by his on-and-off Sufism. Here is the largest collection of his poems in English in book form, in the correct rhyme-structure and meaning. Introduction on his life, times & poetry and the forms he wrote in. 183 pages.

>THE POETRY OF INDIA<
Anthology of Poets of India from 3500 B.C. to the 20th century
Translations, Introductions... Paul Smith

India has a great tradition of poetry over the past 5,500 years. From the *Ramayana* of Valmiki through to the *Bhakti* and Sufi poets and those of the recent past, its poetry is surely unique. Here for the first time is the largest anthology of all India's greatest poets, poems in the correct rhyme-structure and meaning to be studied and loved in all their beauty and spiritual significance. Here are over 100 of India's greatest poets, many of them women, including... Valmiki, Vyasa, Kalidasa, Appar, Andal, Mas'ud Sa'd, Jayadeva, Mu'in, Baba Farid, Amir Khusrau, Hasan Dihlavi, Jana Bai, Namdev, Dnyaneshwar, Lalla Ded, Vidyapati, Chandidas, Kabir, Nanak, Surdas, Babur, Mira Bai, Ghazali, Tulsidas, Eknath, Akbar, Dadu, Rasakhan, Urfi, Naziri, Qutub Shah, Sa'ib, Kalim, Dara Shikoh, Sarmad, Tukaram, Sultan Bahu, Nasir Ali, Ramdas, Bahina Bai, Makhfi, Vemana, Wali, Bedil, Bulleh Shah, Shah Latif, Ali Haider, Sauda, Dard, Nazir, Mir, Sachal Sarmast, Aatish, Zauq, Ghalib, Dabir, Anees, Shefta, Henry Derozio, Dagh, Farid, Shad, Tagore, Iqbal, Puran Singh, Inayat Khan, Jigar, Huma. Introduction on The Main Forms in the Poetry of India. Pages... 622.

BHAKTI POETRY OF INDIA
An Anthology
Translations & Introductions Paul Smith

Bhakti is the love felt by the worshipper towards the personal God. While *bhakti* as designating a religious path is already a central concept in the *Bhagavad Gita*, it rises to importance in the medieval history of Hinduism, where the *Bhakti Movement* saw a rapid growth of *bhakti* beginning in Southern India with the Vaisnava Alvars (6th-9th century) and Saiva

Nayanars (5th-10th century), who spread *bhakti* poetry and devotion throughout India by the 12th-18th century. The *Bhakti* movement reached North India in the Delhi Sultanate. After their encounter with the expanding religion of Islam and especially Sufism, *bhakti* proponents, who were traditionally called 'saints,' encouraged individuals to seek personal union with the divine. Its influence also spread to other religions. THE POETS: Appar, Andal, Jayadeva, Janabai, Namdev, Dnaneshwar, Lalla Ded, Vidyapati, Chandidas, Kabir, Nanak, Surdas, Mira Bai, Tulsidas, Eknath, Dadu, Rasakhan, Tukaram, Ramdas, Bahina Bai. Introduction on *Bhakti* & the *Bhakti* Poets of India & The Main Forms in the *Bhakti* Poetry of India. The correct rhyme-structure and meaning is here in these poems. Pages 236.

SAYINGS OF KRISHNA
A DAYBOOK
Translation & Introduction Paul Smith
These 366 wise, powerful, loving, enlightened and still totally relevant saying are from the *Bhagavad Gita,* a 700-verse Hindu scripture that is part of the ancient Sanskrit epic, the *Mahabharata,* but is frequently treated as a freestanding text, and in particular as an *Upanishad* in its own right, one of the several books that constitute general Vedic tradition. It is revealed scripture in the views of Hindus, the scripture for Hindus represents the words and message of God, the book is considered among the most important texts in the history of literature and philosophy. The teacher of the *Bhagavad Gita* is Lord Krishna, who is revered by Hindus as a manifestation of God (Parabrahman) Himself, and is referred to as Bhagavan, the Divine One. His sayings are in answers to questions asked by Arjuna, a disciple, on the eve of a battle. "I have revealed to you the Truth, the Mystery of mysteries. Having thought it over, you are free to act as you will." Pages 376.

~CLASSIC POETRY OF AZERBAIJAN~
~An Anthology~
Translation & Introduction Paul Smith
Here is one of the few anthologies in English of the greatest poets of Azerbaijan in the classic period, from the 11th to the 17th century. All the poems translated here in the forms of the *ghazal, masnavi, ruba'i, qit'a* and *qasida* have been kept to the correct rhyme and meaning. The poets are… Qatran, Mahsati, Mujir, Khaqani, Nizami, Shabistari, Humam, Kadi Buran-ud-din, Nasim Anwar, Nesimi, Khata'i, Fuzuli and Sa'ib. There is an Introduction on Various Forms in the Classical Poetry of Azerbaijan

and biographies and further reading options on all of these always engrossing and powerful, beautiful, mysterious, often romantic and spiritual and often Sufi poets. Included is the female poet Mahsati, one of the greatest poets of the east and Nizami, one of the greatest poets of all time. 231 pages.

MANSUR HALLAJ: THE TAWASIN
(Book of the Purity of the Glory of the One)
Translation & Introduction Paul Smith
The Perfect Master, poet & martyr, Husayn Mansur al-Hallaj (died 919), was born near Shiraz and was tortured and executed in Baghdad for declaring: "I am the Truth (Anal Haq)." Much has been written about his famous (and infamous) statement and his masterpiece The Tawasin in which he makes it. 'Written in rhymed Arabic prose… it sets forth a doctrine of saintship—a doctrine founded on personal experience and clothed in the form of a subtle yet passionate dialectic.' R.A. Nicholson. The Introduction here contains: The Life, Times and Works of Mansur Hallaj, The Perfect Master (Qutub), 'Anal-Haq' or 'I am the Truth' of Mansur Hallaj, Four Master Poets of Baghdad who influenced Hallaj and A Selection of Poetry from the Persian, Turkish, Pushtu & Urdu Poets about or influenced by Mansur Hallaj. Appendix: The Story of Idris (Azazil) and Adam From 'The Book of Genesis' of Shahin of Shiraz. This is a free-form poetic translation that captures the beauty, meaning, profundity of this classic of Sufism. Pages 264.

MOHAMMED
In Arabic, Sufi & Eastern Poetry
Translation & Introduction by Paul Smith
Here is a collection of poems from the time of Prophet Mohammed in the 7th century into the 20th century about him and in praise of him by some of the greatest poets writing in Arabic, Persian, Turkish and Urdu of all time, most of them Sufis. The Koran itself like the books of most great Spiritual Masters was in poetry as were the sayings of Jesus, Krishna, Rama, Zarathustra. There is an Introduction on Prophecy & Poetry and on the various forms of poetry used by the poets in this anthology. Included in this anthology are complete translations of the famous three Qasidas of the Prophet's Mantle. THE POETS (in order of appearance): Ka'b ibn Zuhair, Abu Sa'id, Firdausi, Baba Kuhi, Abu Maydan, Nizami, Mu'inuddin Chishti, Ibn 'Arabi, Rumi, Al-Busiri, Sadi, Shabistari, Yunus Emre, Hafiz, Haydar, Nesimi, Suleyman Chelibi, Shah Ni'matu'llah, Fuzuli, Qutub Shah, Makhfi, Hayati, Aatish, Iqbal, Ahmed Shawqi. Pages 254.

GITA GOVINDA
The Dance of Divine Love of Radha & Krishna
>Jayadeva<
Translation by Puran Singh & Paul Smith
Jayadeva (circa 1200 AD.) was a Sanskrit poet and most known for his immortal composition, the epic poem/play *Gita Govinda* that depicts the divine love of Avatar Krishna and his consort, Radha. This poem is considered an important text in the Bhakti (Path of Love) movement of Hinduism. The work delineates the love of Krishna for Radha, the milkmaid, his faithlessness and subsequent return to her, and is taken as symbolical of the human soul's straying from its true allegiance but returning at length to the God that created it. It elaborates the eight moods of the heroine that over the years has been an inspiration for many paintings, compositions and choreographic works in Indian classical dances. It has been translated to many languages and is considered to be among the finest examples of Sanskrit poetry. Paul Smith has worked with Puran Singh's powerful & beautiful original free-form poetic version and brought it up to date. Introduction on Life & Times & Poetry of Kayadeva. Glossary. Pages 107.

GREAT WOMEN MYSTICAL POETS OF THE EAST
~ A Daybook ~
Translation & Introduction by Paul Smith
Here is an enlightened Daybook of 366 inspirational poems by the greatest Women Mystical & Sufi poets of the East from Arabia, Persia, Turkey and India of all time in the forms of the *ruba'i, ghazal masnavi, qi'ta* and others. THE POETS: Rabi'a of Basra, Rabi'a Balkhi, Mahsati, Lalla Ded, Jahan Khatun, Makhfi, Fitnet, Leyla Khanim, Tahirah, Hayati, Parvin. The correct form and meaning has been kept in all of these spiritual and romantic and social poems. Introduction on the various forms of poetry used. 385 pages.

~SUFI LOVE POETRY~ An Anthology
Translation & Introduction Paul Smith
CONTENTS: Sufis: Their Art and Use of Poetry… The Main Forms in Arabic, Persian, Turkish, Kashmiri, Hindi, Urdu, Punjabi, Sindhi, Pushtu & English Sufi Love Poetry… Glossary. THE POETS…Majnun, Rabi'a of Basra, Dhu'l-Nun, Bayazid Bistami, Al Nuri, Junaid, Sumnun, Mansur Hallaj, Ibn 'Ata, Rudaki, Shibli, Baba Tahir, Abu Said, Baba Kuhi, Ansari, Al-Ghazzali, Hamadani, Sana'i, Gilani, Mahsati, Khaqani, Mu'in,

Suhrawadi, Nizami, Ruzbiha, Baghdadi, 'Attar, Auhad-ud-din Kermani, Kamal ud-din, Ibn al-Farid, Ibn 'Arabi, Baba Farid, Hamavi , Baba Afzal, Rumi, Imami, Sadi, 'Iraqi, Sultan Vala, Humam, Yunus Emre, Shabistari, Amir Khusrau, Hasan Dihlavi, Simnani, Auhadi, Khaju, Obeyd Zakan, Emad, Lalla Ded, Hafiz, Jahan Khatun, Ruh Attar, Haydar, Junaid Shirazi, Ahmedi, Kadi Burhan-ud-din, Kamal, Maghribi, Nesimi, Sheykhi, Kasim Anwar, Shah Ni'matu'llah, Shah Da'i, Kabir, Jami, Baba Fighani, Pir Sultan, Khayali, Fuzuli, Urfi, Qutub Shah, Mirza, Nef'i, Sa'ib, Dara Shikoh, Sarmad, Khushal, Sultan Bahu, Ashraf Khan, Makhfi, Bedil, Abdul-Khadir, Rahman Baba, Khwaja Mohammad, Hamid, Wali, Bulleh Shah, Shah Latif, Mushtaq, Ali Haider, Sauda, Dard, Ahmad Shah, Shaida, Nazir Akbarabadi, Hatif, Mir, Sachal Sarmast, Galib, Bibi Hayati, Rida 'Ali Shah, Esrar Dede, Aatish, Tahirah, Farid, Shad, Khusrawi, Iqbal, Inayat Khan, Ashgar, Jigar , Khadim, Huma, Veysel, Firaq, Josh, Paul. Pages 560.

THE BHAGAVAD GITA: The Gospel of the Lord Shri Krishna
Translated from original Sanskrit with Introduction by Shri Purohit Swami
General Introductions and to Chapters by Charles Johnston
Revised into Modern English with an Introduction by Paul Smith
The Bhagavad Gita is the single most famous poem in the ancient literature of India. It is equally celebrated as the highest spiritual philosophy and poetry. It constitutes the beginning and in a sense the end of any true knowledge of Indian mysticism. The translator refers to it as 'The Bible of India'. The Guardian said of this translation in 1935 when it was first published: "A beautiful rendering, and gives the reader a clearer and more truthful impression of what the Indian reader takes it to mean than a literal translation would do." Illustrated. 326 pages.

ZARATHUSHTRA: SELECTED POEMS
A New Verse Translation and Introduction by Paul Smith
from the Original Translation by D.J. Irani.
Original Introduction by Rabindranath Tagore.
The Perfect Master and Prophet and one of the first poets Zarathushtra (Zoroaster) lived approx. 7000 B.C. and through his teaching of 'Good words, good thoughts, good deeds' brought in his poems that are similar in form to ruba'is a revelation and dispensation of Divinity. His teaching and poetry have influenced most religions that followed and his poems/songs were a great influence on many of the Sufi poets, including Rumi. Here are 116 of his profound, simple, inspiring poems selected from the Gathas. 141 pages.

THE DHAMMAPADA: The Gospel of the Buddha
Revised Version by Paul Smith
from translation from the Pali of F. Max Muller

From ancient times to now, the Dhammapada has been regarded as the
most succinct expression of the Buddha's teaching and the chief spiritual
testament of early Buddhism. In the countries following Buddhism, the
influence of the Dhammapada is immeasurable. It is a guidebook for
resolving problems of everyday life, and a primer for the instruction in the
wisdom of understanding. The admiration the Dhammapada has elicited
has not been confined to followers of Buddhism. Wherever it has become
known, its moral earnestness, realistic understanding of human life, wisdom
and stirring message of a way to freedom from suffering have won for it the
devotion and veneration of those responsive to the good and the true. 247
pages

THE YOGA SUTRAS OF PATANJALI
"The Book of the Spiritual Man" An Interpretation By Charles Johnston
General Introduction by Paul Smith

The Yoga Sutras of Patanjali are 194 Indian *sutras* (aphorisms) that
constitute the foundational text of Raja Yoga. Yoga is one of the six
orthodox schools of Hindu philosophy. Various authorities attribute the
compilation to Patanjali 2nd century BCE. In the Yoga Sutras, Patanjali
prescribes adherence to eight 'limbs' or steps to quiet one's mind and
liberation. The Sutras not only provide yoga with a thorough and consistent
philosophical basis, they also clarify many important esoteric concepts that
are common to all traditions of Indian thought, such as *karma*. Pages 173

POETRY

THE MASTER, THE MUSE & THE POET
An Autobiography in Poetry by… Paul Smith

Born in Melbourne, Australia, in 1945, Paul Smith began composing poems
in the ancient Persian form of the *ghazal* at the age of 6 on his way to
school. Here are most of his poems composed over the past 45 years… free-
form, rhyming, *ruba'is, ghazals, masnavis* etc. Here are poems composed at
home or travelling in the East and the U.S.A while giving readings of his
poetry and translations. Here are poems of a personal nature, about human
love & grief, about evolution and God and man and the environment and
the past, present and future. Many of the poems were composed while
translating the works of Hafiz, Sadi, Nizami, Rumi, Kabir, Obeyd Zakani,

Jahan Khutan and many others and while writing novels, screenplays and plays where he continued to tell the inner and outer story of his passage through this mysterious and wonderful and sometimes very painful life. 637 Pages.

~A BIRD IN HIS HAND~
POEMS FOR AVATAR MEHER BABA
1967 – 2007… by Paul Smith

On a ship leaving Bombay for Italy in 1965 the Author met a man who had just met the Indian born Perfect Spiritual Master of Iranian descent Meher Baba, (Merwan S. Irani). After a year investigating his life and teaching he accepted him as his Spiritual Master in 1966, and from his books heard of the Persian poet of *ghazals,* Hafiz of Shiraz, whom many believed (including Meher Baba) was the greatest poet that ever lived but had not been adequately translated into English. While working on translating the poetry of Hafiz, Kabir, Sadi and many other Master Poets for the past forty years he has continued to compose his own poems and this book is a compilation of most of those (except for *Compassionate Rose* and *Pune: The City of God)* that are dedicated to his Spiritual Master, Meher Baba. 424 pages.

~THE ULTIMATE PIRATE~ (and the Shanghai of Imagination)
A FABLE
by Paul Smith

This long poem and the poems related to it were composed in 1973 while translating *'Divan* of Hafiz'. The author had read Meher Baba's masterpiece 'God Speaks' that explained everything and in particular, the inner planes of consciousness… of which this is an imagined fable about such a journey. His 'Creative Imagination' at the time was so acute and deep that the journey at times seemed so real that he passed out from the bliss that he was experiencing. Since a child he had always loved pirate movies and to a certain extent in this poem he pays homage to them through the Ultimate Pirate, this time, his Spiritual Master, Meher Baba. Illustrations by Oswald Hall. 157 pages.

+THE CROSS OF GOD+
A Poem in the *Masnavi* Form
by Paul Smith

The *masnavi* is the form used in Persian, Turkish, Urdu and other poetry to write epic ballads or romances and is essentially a Persian invention. Each couplet has a different rhyme with both lines rhyming. This is to allow the

poet greater freedom to go into a longer description of the subject he has chosen to present. All of the great, long, narrative poems of Persia were composed in this form that is not known in classical Arabic poetry. The most famous poems written in this form are the 'Shahnama' (Book of the Kings) of Firdausi, the 'Enclosed Garden of the Truth' of Sana'i, the 'Five Treasures' of Nizami, the 'Conference of the Birds' and 'The Book of God' and many others by 'Attar, the 'Seven Thrones' of Jami, the ten *masnavis* of Amir Khusraw and of course the great *'Masnavi'* of Rumi. Here is a *masnavi* by poet and translator Paul Smith based on the following from Isaiah 53: "It is certain, the cross could not have existed without the efforts of Jesus, who is responsible for the tree, the nails & the tools that fashioned the cross; as well as the materials that fashioned the scourge, which caused His suffering."
It explores with much beauty and insight the relationship between an extraordinary father and son and one's spiritual responsibility. It is a long poem for the purity inside of each of us. (7x10 inches).

CRADLE MOUNTAIN
Paul Smith
Illustrations – John Adam
In 1970 an Australian poet, Paul Smith, read in a newspaper of the death of a young fellow-poet on Cradle Mountain in Tasmania. He was deeply touched by the young man's fate and immediately began writing a poem in praise of the poet, Stephen Baxter. He contacted a friend, the artist John Adam, who read his poem and was inspired enough to illustrate it. The book was published in a limited edition to good reviews and quickly sold out. Stephen Baxter's family contacted him and told him he had truly captured the life and unfortunate death of the young poet. This newly revised edition is close to that of the original and contains all of John Adam's inspired illustrations. (7x10 inches) Second Edition.

PUNE: THE CITY OF GOD
(A Spiritual Guidebook to the New Bethlehem)
Photographs & Poems by Paul Smith
In 1985 the author began to feel the need (usually on the site, or shortly afterwards) to put pen to paper and express in free-form, internally-rhyming poetry... a kind of descriptive inner and outer guide to each 'Baba place' in Meher Baba's birth-place of Pune, as he was experiencing it... a 'feeling' of the presence of the Master from the past that was still available... and, (having gone back often to many of the places and discovered this)... the future. He began to take photographs of the places at the same time,

sometimes even in the middle of writing the poem. Interestingly, often when he read these poems to others they inspired them to visit Pune and see and experience Meher Baba's presence in these places for themselves. 200 pages

FICTION

THE FIRST MYSTERY.
A Novel of the Road...
by Paul Smith
THE FIRST MYSTERY is a novel that operates on a number of levels: it is a search, a tracking down of a murderer and a mystery as to who did it. It is a search through many mysterious lands, people and events. Travel Australia, Singapore, Malaysia, Thailand, Cambodia, Laos, Burma, Nepal, Tibet, Kashmir, India and San Francisco. It is a search (through dreams and visions) into the sub-conscious mind of the private detective Dave, representing the cynical westerner, who seeks but is unaware of the true nature of his journey. It is also the story of the other main characters, Johnny Wilkulda an Australian aboriginal tracker who represents the intuitive side of humankind, seeking a higher truth for himself and all others; and Robinson, the 'LSD Professor', who has taken the road of mind-expanding drugs, the 'fast road'. Meet Evie Rush, too beautiful to be a murderer? Meet Collins the murderous homicide detective; meet Arla, the beautiful jazz singer in big trouble in Bangkok; meet Margaret, haunted, looking for love in a rubber plantation in Malaysia; meet the Cambodian Prince in love with music, trying to stop war entering his country; meet Meera the Indian girl, stuck in a whorehouse in Laos and seeing visions of a new Messiah. Meet them and many other strange and fabulous, weird and wonderful characters in THE FIRST MYSTERY, a new kind of novel. 541 pages

~THE HEALER AND THE EMPEROR~
A Historical Novel Based on a True Story
by Paul Smith
Monsieur Ferrier, lifelong friend of extraordinary poet, composer, linguist, author, mystic and healer... Fabre D'Olivet stands at his gravesite. Ferrier remembers Fabre's strange encounter with the unforgettable Chrisna, Le Revolution and the influence of libertines Sigault and his sister Amelie until the destinies of the future healer and emperor collide in 1800 when Napoleon seizes power and Fabre criticises him. After a bizarre assassination attempt Napoleon imprisons him. Before imprisonment Fabre has met his 'muse', the beautiful and mysterious Julie Marcel. Napoleon

has married *his* muse… the older, cold-hearted and envious Josephine, 'The *only* muse in France'. After conquering most esoteric sciences and languages including the extinct ancient Hebrew, Fabre pens among many other unique works his masterpiece *The Hebraic Tongue Restored and The True Translation of Genesis.* But, to get published in 1811 he has to confront his old nemesis, Napoleon. He must prove the miraculous nature of his discovery of the essence of sound and language. He convinces a congenital deaf-mute's mother to let him try to heal him and after four days is successful! A miracle! Napoleon has him arrested after he cures another and the conflict between the healer and the emperor resumes. This time the lives and hearing of many others are at stake in this novel of an extraordinary true story! Pages 149.

>>>GOING<<<BACK…
A Novel by Paul Smith

GOING BACK is a novel inspired by a true story of love, courage and determination set in a land at peace, Australia; and a land at war… Cambodia. It is the story of people made into refugees by war: the orphans, the old, the young and those who have lost everything and the effect that deadly landmines often have on them. It is the story of the few from America and Australia who stand up to help and love and befriend and help them. But it is mostly the amazing true story of one man who rises out of the depth of despair and through a stroke of good fortune sets off on an odyssey into a living hell and by his inventiveness and sense of humour many lives are saved and changed. Unlike other stories set in Vietnam and Cambodia that tell of war from the soldiers point of view, GOING BACK tells the tale of an ordinary man and people who act extraordinarily in the worst kinds of situations. It is a story from the recent past that could have been ripped from the headlines of today and probably tomorrow. It is an important story, a sad, funny, weird, fantastic, awful, heroic story of war and love and peace and friendship that has to be told. 164 pages.

CHILDREN'S FICTION

PAN OF THE NEVER-NEVER
by Paul Smith

Pan is awoken, after sleeping for over a 100 years, in the great wilderness of Wilson's Promontory, Australia (the real Never-Never Land) by a police helicopter searching for Brad Becker, escaped from a children's home outside Wonthaggi, operated by the abusive Mr. Harvey. Pan meets Brad who can't believe who he is but after a fast flight changes his mind. Pan needs help to dig out the lost boys old hide-out. While Brad snoozes, Pan flies over the area to check on the changes while he slept and is happy to have an encounter with the 'Pirates' motorcycle gang unloading drugs from a yacht. Pan flies Brad by night to the Children's Home to bring back Brad's friends … a new lot of 'lost boys'. But there's a snag in the guise of Sandy and Kym. Girls! The other gang members are little Danny who has discovered who Pan really is, Greg, the tractor driver; Mario, an Italian kid and Ben, an Aborigine who amazingly converses with Pan in his mother tongue. Pan flies Sandy down to check out the yacht and search for the 'Pirates' but Pan and Sandy are outsmarted and find themselves all tied up ready to become the sharks breakfast! The others break through to the "lost boys" old hide-out! They discover Pan's strange diary and flashes of his life over 2340 years open up to them as the adventure continues… but, where are Pan and Sandy? 126 pages.

~HAFIZ~
The Ugly Little Boy who became a Great Poet
by Paul Smith
HAFIZ is the true story of the ugliest boy of his age but with a remarkable memory whose father dies when he is eight and he has to live with his mother at his Uncle Sadi's house. Hafiz goes to work in a drapery shop where he becomes part of the people's overthrowing of a cruel ruler. He then becomes an apprentice baker, who delivers bread to the rich suburbs of Shiraz, Persia in 1320. One day he catches sight of Nabat, the beautiful daughter of one of the cities wealthy traders, promised to a handsome prince. Hafiz pours his love into his poems/songs dedicated to her. His words are so wondrous that the greatest minstrel of the day Hajji, takes up his instrument and serenades his loved one for him. His experiences with his Spiritual Master, Attar, and his songs and poems soon establish Hafiz as a force for truth and beauty through his much loved Shiraz, ravaged by wars and revolutions. Fame doesn't come easily as the ruthless rulers and priests conspire to silence the ever-increasing power of Hafiz's voice. Will he and Nabat and his friends like the jester Obeyd and the minstrel Hajji survive? Can words of love defeat hate's sword? Will Hafiz gain his heart's desire? 195 pages.

Made in the USA
Lexington, KY
10 January 2018